Ruth-Ellen Wallace

ALL MY LOVE
ALL MY LIFE

A Devotional for Women

ALL MY LOVE, ALL MY LIFE
Copyright © 2015 by Ruth-Ellen Wallace
Second printing: August, 2022

All rights reserved. Neither this publication nor any part of this publication may be reproduced or transmitted in any form or by any means, electronic or mechanical, including photocopying, recording or any information storage and retrieval system, without permission in writing from the author.

Unless otherwise indicated, all scripture taken from the Holy Bible, NEW INTERNATIONAL VERSION®, NIV® Copyright © 1973, 1978, 1984, 2011 by Biblica, Inc.® Used by permission. All rights reserved worldwide. NEW INTERNATIONAL VERSION® and NIV® are registered trademarks of Biblica, Inc. Use of either trademark for the offering of goods or services requires the prior written consent of Biblica US, Inc. • Scripture quotations marked ISV are taken from The Holy Bible: International Standard Version. Release 2.0, Build 2015.02.09. Copyright © 1995-2014 by ISV Foundation. ALL RIGHTS RESERVED INTERNATIONALLY. Used by permission of Davidson Press, LLC. • Scripture quotations marked (NLT) are taken from the Holy Bible, New Living Translation, copyright © 1996, 2004, 2007 by Tyndale House Foundation. Used by permission of Tyndale House Publishers, Inc., Carol Stream, Illinois 60188. All rights reserved. • Scripture quotations marked (NKJV) or "New King James Version" are taken from the New King James Version / Thomas Nelson Publishers, Nashville: Thomas Nelson Publishers, Copyright ©1982. Used by permission. All rights reserved. • Scripture quotations marked (ESV) are taken from The Holy Bible, English Standard Version (ESV) is adapted from the Revised Standard Version of the Bible, copyright Division of Christian Education of the National Council of the Churches of Christ in the U.S.A. All rights reserved.

ISBN: 978-1-4866-2323-5

Word Alive Press
119 De Baets Street Winnipeg, MB R2J 3R9
www.wordalivepress.ca

Cataloguing in Publication information may be obtained through Library and Archives Canada

DEDICATION

Looking back to my grandmother, Mildred Ruth McKee Wallace,
whom I wish I had the chance to have known.
Your legacy of elegance lives on to inspire me.

Looking forward to all women reading this book, who long for greater
meaning in life. May you find your inner beauty in Christ.

Table of Contents

Author's Welcome   ix
Introduction   xi

January   1
A Journal for the Journey
A Consuming Fire
The Joy Quilt
Living a Responsive Life
The Cup of Faith

February   15
The Five Love Languages:
God's Grace to Us, Our Worship to Him
The Five Love Languages: Words of Affirmation
The Five Love Languages: Quality Time
The Five Love Languages: Physical Touch

March   31
The Five Love Languages: Gifts
The Five Love Languages: Acts of Service
The Five Love Languages: Practicing a Worship Spectrum
For His Name's Sake: Reflections on Psalm 23
Midwives of the Soul

April   51
Scuba Faith
Called to Creativity
Creational Rhythm

Owning Versus Stewarding
The Power of Words

MAY 69

The Mary-Martha Balance
Mothers & Mentors
For Such a Time as This: The Esther Effect
The Proverbial Woman: Reflections on Proverbs 31
The Autograph

JUNE 85

Roses: Soft Blooms, Sharp Thorns
Beauty Has No Worry Warts
Daddy's Girl
Father's Day
Radiant Beauty

JULY 101

The Alabaster Box
Living the Image
Babies Change Everything
Family Generations
Intimacy & Identity

AUGUST 115

The Hidden Treasure
Life at the Altar
The Hope Chest
The Bridegroom is Coming
The Wedding Supper

SEPTEMBER 133

Ruth's Redemption
Honour & Shame
Healing Tears

Your Shield
Reaching Versus Touching:
Measuring Impact God's Way

OCTOBER 155
The Lighthouse
Salt & Light
Scars
Pearls
Our Unchanging God

NOVEMBER 171
The Jeweled Garment
Forgiven? Forgive
The Sword of Prayer
A Beautiful Exchange
Your Crowns in Christ

DECEMBER 189
If Shakespeare Was Jesus
The Magi Mystery
Life As We Know It
Give My Heart
Fit For a King

ORIGINAL POEMS 201
RECOMMENDED READING 205
ABOUT THE AUTHOR 207

Author's Welcome

Thank you for purchasing this devotional! I'm excited to walk through this next year with you. I designed each entry to be read in a certain month, but feel free to read them in any order, using the Table of Contents to find the specific insightful message that speaks to your heart today. I also intend each entry to be read on a Sunday, as a means of quieting the heart on the Lord's Day and as preparation for the coming week. Take the time to look up the Scripture passages in your Bible that I quote, and then read them over again as you journal during the following week. Journaling can be such a rewarding discipline, and so I encourage you to record your plans, prayers, feelings and fears each week and at the end of each month as a way of releasing them to God. At the end of the year, you'll be amazed at how many fears were dispelled and prayers answered!

Though this method will allow the book to be used to its greatest advantage, feel free to read through it faster or slower as you wish. I certainly don't have all the answers – so more than anything I want these weekly insights to inspire you to deep and meaningful conversation with God directly.

I pray that one year from now, you will look back with grateful tears of joy on what the Lord has done in your life and how you have grown in your love for Him. May He have all your love, all your life!

In Him,

Ruth-Ellen

INTRODUCTION

I am sitting here in silence, and yet it is anything but silent. There is the ticking of the clock. The beating of my heart. The constant reminder of a linear reality I know as time. I am restrained to live moment-by-moment, never being able to experience the past or future out of its programmed sequence. And yet my spirit is aware of both. I have memories of the past. Dreams of the future. Longings for fulfillment that I know are impossible to realize in this life. Why?

As I close my eyes, my awareness is heightened. The air I breathe sustains me even though it is invisible. The living cells in my body continue to function and perform even though they are too small to see. My thoughts and emotions still direct my mind and soul even though they are not of a tangible material. Truly, humans are more than just physical objects, and more than just what can be researched scientifically. Yet the scope and span of our intangible faculties are still limited to the physical realm. When our physical body dies, life and reality as we have known it comes to an end, leaving behind grief and longings unfulfilled. Why?

As I sit here alone, I reflect on the people who live in other parts of the world and have very different lives. Different climates, different governments, different cultures, different beliefs. Those who have more than me, and those who have far less. I will never meet most of them or hear the cries of their hearts, and yet I am aware of them and feel connected to them. Why?

I believe these questions can only be answered through a faith connection to an eternal reality that transcends the physical. Though currently we are limited to one space and one time, our Creator isn't, and He made us in His image. Realizing who He has created us to be has everything to do with recognizing these facets of that image in us and meditating on them, recognizing that it will be a limited glimpse at best.

And then there is Jesus. The intangible, eternal Word of God taking on human flesh, with all its limitations of space and time that we experience on Earth. Why? Why would God reduce and debase His Word to our level? In a word, love. For God our Creator is also God our *Father* – a relationship connection as vast and enduring as space and time itself. He knew we needed a Savior and Champion to both redeem us from our sin and blaze a trail for our abundant living, and so He sent Jesus. Only through great love for us does this make any sense. Our sin had hopelessly severed this relationship connection, but Jesus' death paid the sin penalty and restored us to the Father once again.

How, then, shall you respond? If all of this is true, how will you spend all your love, and all your life? If you feel a tug on your heart right now and you would like to receive this free gift of God's love, all you have to do is ask Him in a short prayer:

> Dear Father God,
> Thank you for creating me in Your image.
> I'm sorry for the things I've done in my life
> that have separated me from You.
> Please forgive me, heal me and make me clean.
> Thank you for your gift of salvation through Jesus.
> I invite you now into my heart
> and dedicate to you all my love, for all my life.
> Amen.

If you prayed this simple prayer and meant it in your heart, your newly restored relationship connection with the Father has just begun! The next step is to tell someone about this decision you've just made, and then find a church and a Bible that will help teach you more about Jesus. For now, though, I hope you will read through the rest of this book with your heart open to what God wants to say to you. He loves you so much and wants you to know Him more!

January

A Journal for the Journey

Life is a journey. The path we are given to walk is narrow, steep, rocky, and winding. It may even be obscured in response to the changing seasons: by snow in the winter, mud in the spring, weeds in the summer, and leaves in the fall. We may grow weary, frustrated, or angry along the way, and certainly older. The one thing that remains constant is God. Our constant Companion, Helper, Provider, and Sustainer, we walk this road of change with the One who never changes.

I have designed this devotional book as a journal. Whether or not you've ever enjoyed putting your thoughts down on paper, I encourage you to try it for a year. Journaling is a great way for us as women to deposit our daily thoughts, fears, emotions and prayers in a place outside of ourselves where we can return to and reflect on later. There is great meaning to be found in remembrance. The psalmist writes, "I will remember the deeds of the Lord; yes, I will remember your miracles of long ago" (Psalm 77:11, NIV). Rereading a journal much later can be gratifying, painful, or even embarrassing, but it is always instructive. Recognizing prayers answered and worries come to nothing is a big part of it, but primarily journaling should validate that your feelings are important, while also demonstrating the stark contrast between your heart's tidal waves of emotion and the still calmness of the Lord's faithfulness. Like the psalmist did, when we remember the awesome deeds of God and how He has spoken to us in the past, we are encouraged in the midst of our present storm. Likewise, when we've come through a storm, we can look back with grateful hearts on the saving power of our God. This journey we call life is not supposed to be easy; the call on our lives was never meant to be a walk in the park. Wind, rain, and snow can make the already uneven and steep route almost impossible to travel. Simply put, it is a trail of trial. Yet part of gaining wisdom over the course of the journey is remembering and reflecting on where you've been and what it has taught you.

We live in a competitive, eat-or-be-eaten capitalistic society that seems to show very little care or concern for emotional health. Government programs, fair trade societies, and non-profit organizations make it appear as if we live in a just society that practices compassion, but these are merely band-aid solutions on a much deeper wound. What are people truly in need of? The answer is God. People need to know God's heart for them and the world. We serve a God of immense creativity, strength, beauty and wisdom that I hope this devotional will reveal to you in a more profound way. It is my prayer that you use the questions at the end of each month to inspire you to journal your deepest feelings in a constructive way, offering them up to God in exchange for His heart's cry for you.

That's when the Beautiful Exchange begins. I'm referring to Isaiah 61:3, where God promises to give us "beauty for ashes, the oil of joy for mourning, [and] the garment of praise for the spirit of heaviness." Relationships are always a two-way street. Only when we offer to Him our jumbled pile of need will He give us the beauty, joy and praise that we long for. That's why this narrow path we walk is restricting yet comforting; lonely yet deeply relational; steep yet ascending, winding yet adventurous, painful yet fruitful, rough and rocky yet solid and secure. It's not about where you are, it's Who you're with (and where He's taking you!)

This week, take the time to read Psalm 77 several times, meditate on each verse and reflect on all God has done for you. Then, begin to journal. What are your plans and prayers for this week? Your feelings and fears?

A Consuming Fire

It's winter. Everyone and everything is trying to keep warm amidst frigid temperatures. These days, there's nothing that restores me more than relaxing next to my fireplace after a busy day. This welcoming hearth also reminds me of the enduring heart of God and helps to put life back into perspective.

Indeed, in a controlled environment, fire can be very attractive - so much so that we often forget the inherent danger it possesses. When boundaries are removed, though, fire inevitably spreads quickly to cause destruction and death. It makes all the difference who has control.

The Bible often uses the imagery of fire to teach important principles about God. In Deuteronomy 4:24, we are warned clearly that "the Lord your God is a consuming fire". The Israelites knew very well that this didn't refer to a warm hearth on a cold day; it meant a raging, blazing, spreading inferno. A fearful concept. So many people in today's postmodern world are attracted to the warmth and light of God yet are reluctant to allow Him and His absolute Truth to *consume* them. They prefer to experience the comfort of God in a fireplace, where His warmth can be enjoyed and His burning power controlled. As followers of Jesus, we need to release control back to God - to allow His holy, consuming fire to penetrate our beings so that He can show His power and accomplish His agenda. Wow - that's a tall order. To start, let's explore some of the characteristics of fire.

- Fire brings light. Ephesians 5:8, 11, 13 says "for you were once darkness, but now you are light in the Lord. Live as children of light. Have nothing to do with the fruitless deeds of darkness, but rather expose them. [For] everything exposed by the light becomes visible – and everything that is illuminated becomes a light." Allowing the light from God's fire to completely expose us is a high price to pay for many - we somehow feel entitled to our privacy. Yet if we truly desire God's light to shine out from us, it must penetrate every corner of our heart.

- Fire melts and molds. I know how easy it is to develop a cold, hard heart – bitterness, hurt, and unforgiveness can slowly seep into our lives until all tenderness is gone. God's consuming fire wants to melt your heart back to its original tender state and mold it into the image of Jesus.

- Fire burns. We all enjoy warm weather, and we've all experienced the discomfort of a sunburn when we've enjoyed too much of it. As God's fire melts and molds, it will also burn - burn up our sinful flesh, our selfish desires, our hidden motives. Warning - we're getting pretty close to the heat now; only the truly committed heart will endure. We read about God's Judgement Day in I Corinthians 3:11-13: "For no one can lay any foundation other than the one already laid, which is Jesus Christ. If anyone builds on this foundation using gold, silver, costly stones, wood, hay or straw, their work will be shown for what it is, because the Day will bring it to light. It will be revealed with fire, and the fire will test the quality of each person's work." The substances that can withstand heat, like gold, silver and gems, are the ones that are costly. We need to be prepared to pay a high price in order to further His Kingdom.

- Fire purifies and refines. Even valuable material like gold and silver contain impure elements that need to be removed. Zechariah 13:9 alludes to this: "[My people] I will put into the fire; I will refine them like silver and test them like gold. They will call on my name and I will answer them; I will say, 'They are my people,' and they will say, 'The Lord is our God'." We need to daily ask God to refine our offerings to Him by testing our hearts and burning away anything impure.

- Fire stimulates growth. This is the best part! Just as a prairie fire burns away the overgrowth to return nutrients to the soil for seed germination, you'll begin to experience new *growth* in your life when you allow God's consuming fire to take control. He'll birth dreams and blaze trails that would never have been possible had you confined Him to the fireplace. You also won't be able to stop sparks from flying into the paths of others as you radiate His presence along life's journey - but it won't matter anymore. This fire is now out of your control.

It's still pretty cold out there - but may the below zero temperatures remind us of the state of our hearts, and a world in need of God's consuming fire.

This week, take the time to look up these verses, meditate on them, and then begin to journal. In what areas of your life are you restricting

God to the fireplace? As you journal your plans, prayers, feelings, and fears, lay them down at His feet, asking Him to fill you with a greater trust in His goodness and provision for you.

THE JOY QUILT

Last summer, the Lord laid it on my heart to complete a project that had long been abandoned – not by me, but by my grandmother. Fifteen years prior, my grandma had decided to make a quilt for me. She had made quilts for the other grandkids in previous years, and now my turn had come. I had been given several patterns to choose from, and a choice of colors. I could just picture her busily selecting the fabric at the store, bringing it home and starting to carefully cut out each tiny piece. I can't even imagine how frustrating it must have been when, shortly after beginning my quilt, she was diagnosed with cancer. It was so painful to watch her slowly slip away as she fought bravely for three years until it finally took her life. The unfinished quilt, still in small pieces, was packed up and stored away.

When my parents decided to sell the house I grew up in, the quilt pieces were discovered and handed over to me in the hope that someone, at sometime, would make the effort to complete the project. So last summer, I decided it was time - and it was going to be me who did it.

I had never quilted before, but I knew enough to know that I needed the pattern - and it was missing. How was I supposed to put these pieces together correctly without the pattern? After all attempts had failed at locating it, I decided just to lay out all the pieces on the floor and see what I could make of them. I did purchase a 'how-to' book for beginning quilters, which turned out to be all I needed. As I carefully tried different placements for the pieces, I eventually found an arrangement that I liked and that would also be fairly simple to complete. Following my book step by step, my quilt slowly began to take shape.

I've always enjoyed creating things by hand, especially something new that I never thought I could do before. I felt amazed at the results of my labor, and sentimental at the fact that I was completing something my grandmother had begun. It was a group effort! The tiny fabric pieces she had put so much time into cutting out were finally being unified and given a purpose by my own pattern and my own hand.

Do you think that's how God feels about us? He certainly doesn't enjoy watching us suffer like we do - but how His tremendously creative heart longs to bring redemption and renewed purpose into our random, assorted pieces! The Bible says in Psalm 126:5-6 that "those who sow with tears will reap with songs of joy. Those who go out weeping, carrying seed to sow, will return with songs of joy, carrying sheaves with them." It's never easy having to endure seasons of sorrow and brokenness, but if we remember that they are often necessary to bring joy and harvest, then we can learn to trust God's ultimate plan more as we go through them. And even if you've spent years feeling guilty and regretful about something, it's never too late to bring it all to God. Only He alone knows the ultimate pattern that will bring all your pieces together and have your life showcase His beauty. Like learning to quilt, all we need is the 'how-to' book - the Bible that can take us each step of the way. Leave the big pattern to Him.

Looking back, I'm so glad I took the time and effort to complete my quilt. In fact, I've named it my Joy Quilt. Partly because of Psalm 126:5-6 (I felt I was literally 'sewing' with tears and singing with joy at the same time) but mostly because my grandmother's name was Joyce, and I was given my middle name 'Joy' after her. I hope the quilt will remain useful and beautiful for generations to come, and I can't wait to get to heaven so I can tell grandma how her sacrifice of time and energy was not futile but rather became a symbolic analogy of God's creative redemption.

This week, reflect and journal on what God is redeeming in your life. Ask Him to open your eyes to see His redeeming hand at work, and to unveil the value of something long forgotten that needs bringing in to the light. Then write out your prayer requests, addressing them to Jesus your Redeemer.

Living a Responsive Life

As I write this, the world is returning home from the Winter Olympics. During any Olympics, extensive media coverage constantly preaches the value of competition, striving to be the best, and pursuing your dreams. Yet I wonder. Were humans really created to become so focused on one dream - to be the best - at the exclusion of all other things in life? What about God's dreams for us? Competition can be healthy, of course, so long as it promotes teamwork and develops character, and God often brings athletes to the Olympics to use their influence for His glory. However, the majority of serious Olympic athletes suffer from stress, anxiety, and even depression, which the media fails to report.

We are selfish beings by nature, and our constant self-awareness and self-preservation clouds our view of what is really going on in the world around us. That's why Romans 12:2 is so crucial to memorize and take to heart: "Do not be conformed to this world, but be transformed by the renewing of your mind, that you may prove what is that good and acceptable and perfect will of God." Did you catch that last part? The perfect will of God. It's really all about Him. God is the only true *active* force in this world, and us created humans are meant to be *responsive*. Not active, not passive, but responsive. The key to everything is this: "This is love: not that we loved God, but that he loved us and sent his Son as an atoning sacrifice for our sins" (I John 4:10).

Living responsively is such a foreign concept to our modern way of thinking. For me, I like to remind myself regularly that we as the church are the bride of Christ, and meditate on what that really means. In Jesus' day, the groom did everything to prepare for his wedding. He not only pursued the bride, but also made all the preparations for the wedding day and for their future home. The bride's job was to *wait and be ready when the groom called for her*. So it is with us. You may not feel that God is moving in your life but continue to remain faithful and trust Him. As His bride, He is actively pursuing you, defending you and preparing you for what *He* dreams for you to be, and asks for you to *respond* to Him. He knows your every need and always has your best interests at heart.

Still feeling lonely and fearful? Remember, God is also the Creator of relationship. He formed the mountains, trees, and the air we breathe, but His favourite creative work is people. He takes his greatest delight in molding us and bringing us into relationship with Him and with each other. He knows that marriage, family, and community are what cause His love and glory to shine brightest. Not even the most magnificent sunset can compare. Once we focus on unity and relationship - instead of competition - will we start to approach the target. We work best as a team.

Don't get me wrong, I really enjoy watching the Olympics, and celebrating each gold medal! But let's not forget the Lord's desire to see us live united together, humbly responsive to His love.

This week, meditate and journal your feelings of response to God's pursuit of you. As you record your plans and prayers, ask Him to overshadow them with His plans and dreams for you.

THE CUP OF FAITH

Faith is one of those terms that has become cliché, and often separated from its Biblical meaning. We now refer casually to 'having faith' in someone or speaking 'in good faith'. It has become a term of vague optimism and positive thinking, no longer requiring any action on our part. Yet James 2:26 says that "as the body without the spirit is dead, so faith without deeds is dead." So what is faith really?

The closest thing we have in the Bible to a definition of faith is found in Hebrews 11:1. "Now faith is confidence in what we hope for and assurance about what we do not see." This verse highlights two different aspects of faith, like two sides of a coin. First of all, we have faith when we confidently lay claim in our hearts to what is yet to come in the future. When we read the Bible, and confidently believe all the things it says about heaven and the future, we have faith. We also have faith when we are assured of the reality of present things we can't see. If you are a follower of Jesus, the Holy Spirit is inside you right now, guiding you and protecting you, even though you can't see Him. You can have faith by believing in both of these realities, the future one and the invisible one. I like to use the symbol of a cup to demonstrate how these two aspects of faith can work together. An empty cup is an object that carries both a functional promise of future filling, as well as an invisible present fullness. A cup is designed to be filled with something; an obvious potential and purpose even when it is empty. The same is true of ourselves as Christians. Though we have never seen our Savior, our hearts were molded as empty containers that only He can fill, which gives us the faith that it will come to pass. However our empty hearts really aren't truly empty, are they? Right now they contain the Holy Spirit and His invisible attributes, just like a cup holds invisible air when it's not 'full'.

This is all really great to know, but the sad part is that there is so much more to faith that so many people miss. Faith is not faith until it is put into *action*. The remaining verses in Hebrews 11 itemize the faith of various people as demonstrated by their actions. Though their stories and experiences are diverse, they describe three keys that unlock active faith: *obedience, perseverance, and trust*. If we believe the Bible to be true, then there is no getting away from the commands that Jesus gives us to obey. By obeying Him, we can unlock that first gate towards active faith. Once we've taken that first step, we must then persevere on an often difficult road. If faith is truly a conviction of what we do not see, then perseverance must be part of the proof. Finally, active faith requires the key of trust. There will be times of testing, when life is rough and God is silent, that requires us to trust His unseen goodness despite all visible evidence to the contrary. Does having 'faith' now seem a bit daunting to you? It should, particularly if you simply claim to believe the words of the Bible without actually knowing its Author. Truly knowing God is what makes all the difference. When you know God, His very presence will be to you like it was to Abraham and be your "very great reward" (Genesis 15:1). Abraham was promised an incredible homeland and endless descendants, yet the promise coming from God could not be compared to the reward of knowing God. Knowing God was what gave Abraham the courage to *obey* God's call to leave his birthplace. Knowing God gave him the tenacity to *persevere* as a foreigner in Canaan. Knowing God gave him the ability to *trust* as he offered his only son on the altar. So are you prepared to redefine what faith means to you, and to practice obedience, perseverance, and trust? Remember, "we are surrounded by such a great cloud of witnesses, [so] let us run with perseverance the race marked out for us, fixing our eyes on Jesus, the pioneer and perfecter of faith" (Hebrews 12:1-2). These feats of faith are impossible with man, but when you know God, "all things are possible" (Luke 1:37). Let Him fill your cup to overflowing.

This week, take the time to read Hebrews 11, meditating on how the themes of obedience, perseverance and trust are presented. As you journal, write out several bold faith-filled prayers that you are believing God for, asking God to increase your faith for more.

Plans and Prayers

In your journal, take the time to write down your plans and goals for the coming month of February.

What New Year's resolutions are you wanting to keep?

What items on your 'bucket list' do you want to accomplish this year?

What first step could you take right now towards one of them?

Write out some thoughts on what it means to live a life of faith, and the impact it can have on others.

What concerns are on your heart today that you need to write out in faith as prayer requests to the Lord?

What do you need to confess to Him? What can you thank Him for?

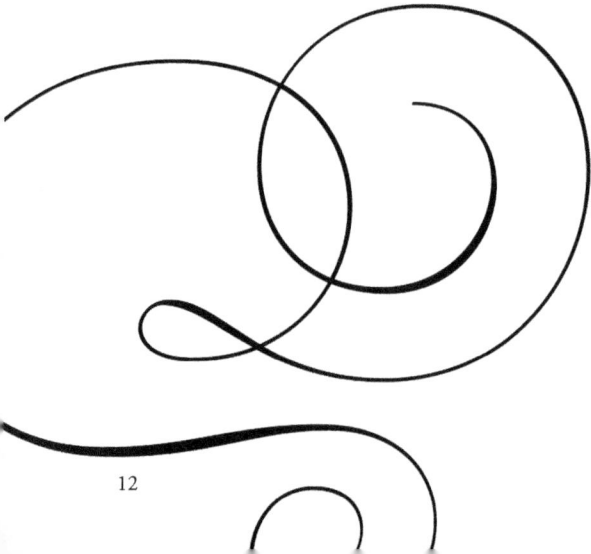

Feelings and Fears

What are you feeling today? Joyful? Burdened? Frustrated? Numb?

In what areas of your life do you feel 'stuck' right now?

Write out how you feel before God: He's been in your shoes and knows what you're going through.

What fears are holding you back from fully obeying and trusting God?

Freely journal whatever comes to mind, as an act of surrendering it all to Him.

FEBRUARY

The Five Love Languages:
God's Grace to Us, Our Worship to Him

What is worship exactly? A dictionary would say that worship is an expression of reverence and adoration for a deity. Yet the dictionary does not give examples of deities, nor examples of expression. As Christians, we believe in one triune God, Father, Son, and Holy Spirit, and the truth of His Word. We read in John 4:24: *"God is spirit, and His worshippers must worship in the Spirit and in truth."* Our means of connection with God is through His Spirit and the truth of His Word, for these are the ways that He first connects with us.

Worship is therefore our love response to God. *"This is love: not that we loved God, but that he loved us and sent his Son as an atoning sacrifice for our sins. Dear friends, since God so loved us, we also ought to love one another. No one has ever seen God, but if we love one another, God lives in us and his love is made complete in us"* (1 John 4:10-11).

This got me to thinking. The ground-breaking book by Gary Chapman, "The Five Love Languages", has revolutionized the way we understand human expressions of love for each other. Yet according to the verse we just read, our expression of love for each other is also an extension of God's love for us and our worship of Him. Therefore could we possibly apply the five love languages directly to our relationship with God? Come along with me as we explore some of the possible applications of this concept, to discover new avenues of worship expression and deeper levels of meaning in those you already practice.

The overall theme of Dr. Chapman's book is that these love languages are expressed in differing amounts from one person to another. In turn, then, our primary language of love will likely be our language of worship, and our primary means of experiencing his love. Yet by pursuing an understanding of all five love languages we can bring greater enrichment and variety to our worship, and more deeply minister to the God who created *all* these things for His glory. So for this week, here are three insights regarding how we worship:

- Worship is a lifestyle. Our days are made up of time spent and words spoken, so how can we make lifestyle changes that better express the love languages of quality time and words of affirmation? First, we must recognize our ongoing, selfish desires for more - more food, more pleasure, more money, more power – and that only through God can we find fulfillment, know contentment, and be satisfied with what we have. A worship lifestyle recognizes His control over all life, and spends life choosing to lay down all desires to put Him first. Matt. 6:33 says, "*Seek first His kingdom and His righteousness, and all these things will be given to you as well.*"

- Worship brings perspective. As we worship in Spirit and Truth, we become more satisfied with what we have, and less satisfied with who we are. We gaze on the holiness of God, and more clearly see the holes in ourselves. Worship also gives us a stronger grasp on His purposes for us, and a stronger desire to use our talents as gifts for His glory.

- Worship reveals identity. Just as an unborn baby's fingerprints are formed through it physically interacting with the womb of its mother, so our unique identity is only fully revealed to us through reaching out to our Creator. The more we do so, the more our hearts become engraved with His Spirit and His Truth, sealing our identity as His child so securely that the enticements of this world fade away.

- Worship is pursuing God's heart. Our needs are so real, and our emotions can be overwhelming. Yet by choosing to worship God within our emotional tidal waves, we recognize that God's constant love is more real still. When praise is a sacrifice, or when He brings us to things requiring obedience, submission, and surrender, we are more fully pursuing His heart. Just as His ways and thoughts are higher than our own, so are the things that break His heart. By stepping out of our own brokenness to bring comfort and hope to a broken world, we worship in the truest form.

So are you ready? Over the next few weeks, we'll be examining the five love languages as five different ways that God communicates His love to us, and how we can use those same five ways to offer worship back to Him. This week, reflect on the Five Love Languages and which ones you resonate with most. Then consider how you best connect to God. Prayer? Singing? Serving others? Dancing? Cooking? Gardening? Building things? As you worship this week, consider what new ways or modes of expression might be equally life-giving to you but serve His heart more fully.

THE FIVE LOVE LANGUAGES:
WORDS OF AFFIRMATION

With the massive amount of messages out there screaming at us every day, a woman needs to have a strong conviction of who she is and who she belongs to. The Word of God is a powerful means of reaffirming and reminding us of the Truth that we can hold on to during our darkest and most painful seasons of doubt and discouragement. *"This means that anyone who belongs to Christ has become a new person. The old life is gone; a new life has begun!"* (2 Corinthians 5:17, NLT). We are now dead to sin and alive in Christ and have been given the freedom to redefine ourselves accordingly. So though you may still make mistakes and experience failure, these things no longer *define* you, for God has given you a new name. "No longer will they call you Deserted or name your land Desolate. But you will be called ["My delight is in her"], and your land ["married"]; for the Lord will take delight in you, and your land will be married. As a young man marries a young woman, so will your Builder marry you; as a bridegroom rejoices over his bride, so will your God rejoice over you" (Isaiah 62:4-5). In Christ, your very identity has been changed from lonely and barren to beloved and fruitful – and no other person or circumstance can ever change that – ever.

As incredible as the words are that God has spoken over us, more incredible still are the words He has given us to describe Him in return. Relationships are about mutual belonging, so God in His grace has not only bestowed on us a new name but has given us glimpses of Himself. We worship God according to how He has revealed Himself to us, which is the grand theme unfolded in the Old Testament. In it, we better understand the nature of His holy character and our idolatrous rebellion; of our spiritual bankruptcy and the lengths to which He has freely chosen to redeem us.

Speaking the redemptive names of God over your life is a powerful tool for both worshipping Him and reaffirming the ways that He is actively restoring and fighting for you as His bride. So declare these over yourself right now: *Jehovah Jireh*, The Lord Will Provide (Genesis 22:14), *Jehovah Rapha*, The Lord is my Healer (Exodus 15:26), *Jehovah Nissi*, The Lord is my Banner (Exodus 17:15), *Jehovah Shalom*, The Lord is my Peace (Judges 6:24), *Jehovah Raha*, The Lord is my Shepherd (Psalm 23:1), *Jehovah Tsitkinu*, The Lord is my Righteous Savior (Jeremiah 23:6), and *Jehovah Shamma*, The Lord is Here (Ezekiel 48:35). What's more, Psalm 23 contains all seven of these names within its poetic structure, so it is a great Psalm to memorize and speak over yourself as you feel the need to be reminded of your true identity and the nature of the God you belong to. For "you are a chosen people, a royal priesthood, a holy nation, God's special possession, that you may declare the praises of him who called you out of darkness into his wonderful light" (1 Peter 2:9).

Yet we must always remember that true worship is about adoring God for who He is in Himself. It has nothing at all to do with you. It is not something we conjure up on Sunday morning with instruments and voices, but rather it is our verbal expression to God of all He is. Your words of affirmation within true worship should primarily reflect the awesome, holy, grandeur of our Mighty King of Love and His innumerable powerful attributes. Yet many of the songs we sing in church place too much emphasis on what *we* feel, say, and do and not as much on who God is in and of Himself. Sure, these songs make us feel good and affirm who we are in Christ, but they are songs of praise and thanksgiving, not worship. Psalm 100:4 says, "Enter his gates with thanksgiving and his courts with praise, give thanks to him and praise his name." We enter into worship through gates of thanksgiving and praise for all He has done, but worship happens on a deeper level. When you are truly encountering the living God, self-awareness vanishes as you gaze upon His glory and majesty. You may feel small and weak, but that is exactly the heart posture true worship requires. For only then do we recognize our ongoing need for Him. Isaiah 64:6 says "all of us have become like one who is unclean, and all our righteous acts are like filthy rags." Even the most generous and loving Christian woman – the Proverbs 31 woman, if you like – has the same desperate need for God as you and I do. The difference is that she is more aware of it. By proclaiming words of pure reverence and adoration to God, we widen the gap between His righteousness and our own and declare our need for what only He can give.

So how could you start to cultivate words of pure worship in your heart? I would suggest reading Revelation 4-7. It is also excellent preparation for how we will be worshipping the Lamb for all eternity. Also, there are many Psalms that solely describe God's attributes: Psalm 105, 111, 113, 135, 146, 147, and particularly Psalm 136. Allow these to lead you into true worship.

Yet I would challenge you to use these Scriptures and the lyrics of worship songs as springboards to using your own personal words of affirmation to God. A former music pastor of mine gave a brilliant illustration many years ago that I've never forgotten: When you receive a store-bought greeting card from someone, there will inevitably be a generic message inscribed inside. As moving, funny or poetic as its lines may be, the card will always take on greater value if the giver took the time to write something personally inside. It's the same with our words of worship and praise to God. It's great to sing the beautifully-scripted words of a worship chorus to Him – an uplifting chord progression paired with majestic lyrics and rhyming stanzas – yet what really touches God is when He hears a unique melody from a fully-surrendered heart that passionately offers its own personal script amidst pain and brokenness. Acknowledging His supreme holiness and wisdom in your own words is like adding your own personal comment to an already beautiful greeting card; it can transform an acquaintance into an intimate friend.

This week, write out Scriptures that declare who you are in Christ, embracing them as God's words of affirmation over you. Then journal your own words of praise and thanksgiving for all He has done for you. Finally, focus your mind and heart on true worship by reading Revelation 4-7. Gaze on his holiness and majesty and let your worship flow.

The Five Love Languages:
Quality Time

All time to God is potential quality time. The greatest longing of His heart is simply to spend time with us. He created time itself as a means of communicating His timeless love. Ecclesiastes 3:11 says, "He has made everything beautiful in its time. He has also set eternity in the human heart; yet no one can fathom what God has done from beginning to end." Our finite minds will never be able to grasp the eternal nature of our soul, only recognize its infinite Provider. "The life of mortals is like grass, they flourish like a flower of the field; the wind blows over it and it is gone, and its place remembers it no more. But from everlasting to everlasting the Lord's love is with those who fear Him" (Psalm 103:15-17). He knows your limitations, particularly your limited amount of time. He knows your daily struggle to address both the urgent tasks and the important relationships. Yet He is always there, inviting you to spend time with Him. His invitation is not an additional demand on your time, but rather a refreshing escape from it. He is saying to you now, "Come to me, you who are weary and burdened, and I will give you rest. Take my yoke upon you and learn from me, for I am gentle and humble in heart, and you will find rest for your soul. For my yoke is easy and my burden is light" (Matthew 11:28-30). Every moment of our lives, each breath we breathe, was given to us by a God who wants us to know Him and enjoy Him always. Isaiah 30:18 says, "The Lord longs to be gracious to you; therefore He will rise up to show you compassion." He wants to help carry your burden of having too much to do in too little time, but you must choose to first be still and listen.

You see, quality time with God is only limited by your own recognition of His constant presence. How His heart must break over every moment that we allow to pass by without acknowledging Him! He laments, "All day long I have held out my hands to an obstinate people, who walk in ways not good, pursuing their own imaginations" (Isaiah 65:2). This is such a poignant image to me: our eternal, powerful Creator reaching his hands out to embrace His children, while they ignore Him, go their own way, fight their own battles, and nurse their own wounds. They commiserate, philosophize, debate, and strive amongst themselves, remaining committed to worshipping only themselves, come what may. When will we realize only God can fix our brokenness? When will we take the time to look up from our futile efforts and see His arms outstretched to us in love? His love is as limitless as the time He wants to spend with you.

Yet God knows our time is limited. In fact, He knows exactly how limited it is. Psalm 139:16 says, "all the days ordained for me were written in your book before one of them came to be." Therefore an important language of worship we can offer Him is our time. Time that we could spend doing something else that we've chosen instead to reserve for Him alone. But how can we make the most out of this time we spend with Him? In other words, how can we be assured of its quality?

The first thing we must do is analyze our motives and the posture of our hearts. Do we approach God only when we want something, or do we simply want to know Him more? Put another way, are you seeking His hands, or are you seeking His face? I like how the acronym A.B.I.D.E. describes this: Accept Being Intimately Dependent on the Lord and Experience His love. Quality time with God involves celebrating and enjoying His presence, just because of who He is and the fact that you belong to Him. There should be no strict schedule, and no hidden agenda. Always be quick to examine yourself for unaddressed sin, worry, fear, doubt, and pride that could tempt you to turn your time together into something selfish and manipulative. James 4:7,8,10 says, "Submit yourselves, then, to God. Resist the devil, and he will flee from you. Come near to God and he will come near to you. Wash your hands, you sinners, and purify your hearts, you double-minded. Humble yourselves before the Lord, and he will lift you up." So enter His presence with a humble spirit of awe and wonder, in reverence of His holiness, and then marvel anew at His grace.

Next, take the time to listen. Be still and know that He is God. Learning how to pray is an important part of our faith development, and we should certainly use the Lord's Prayer, the Psalms, and other Scripture as the basis for what we say to God, yet too often our prayers consist of only us speaking. Our words of worship, thanksgiving, intercession, confession, and petition are crucial and important, but quality time involves two-sided conversation. Read His Word, meditate on its meaning in context, ask Him to speak to you through it, and then prepare yourself to listen.

Finally, are you willing to obey? If after you've read His Word and listened for His voice you've felt the Lord prompt you to make a change in your life, don't conclude your meeting until you have a first step in mind and have committed yourself to seeing it through. God doesn't expect you to have the whole thing figured out, only to take an initial step in faith. Only then will you know if you've truly given your life over to His control.

Lastly, what do you think about 1 Thessalonians 5:17, that challenges us to "pray without ceasing"? We've discussed the quality, so now let's discuss the quantity. Being in constant prayer may seem very impractical to you, with all the tasks you have to do. Shouldn't that verse only apply to nuns and monks and people like that? Yet by reflecting on the characteristics of quality time we're just discussed, perhaps having a humble heart, listening, and being willing to obey could become a lingering state of mind that spills over from your focused quiet time into your entire day's routine. Psalm 89:15-16 says, "Blessed are those who have learned to acclaim you, who walk in the light of your presence, Lord. They rejoice in your name all day long; they celebrate your righteousness." There's no denying that praying without ceasing is something that must be learned, but there's also no denying the great blessing attached to it. This is particularly true when you have an urgent need in your life, for "will not God bring about justice for His chosen ones, who cry out to Him day and night? Will He keep putting them off? I tell you, He will see that they get justice, and quickly" (Luke 18:7-8). These practices, like using words of pure worship, will prepare you for heaven: "[We will be] before the throne of God and serve Him day and night in his temple; and He who sits on the throne will shelter [us] with His presence" (Revelation 7:15). Therefore increasing the quality of the time you spend with God can also increase the time itself, and both will serve to cultivate in us true hearts of worship.

This week, ask yourself: do you regularly include God in your daily agenda, and submit to His guidance and wisdom when making future plans? How often do you take His presence for granted? By making quality time with God a priority, He will fill your days with purpose, meaning, and joy, and give you a grander sense of perspective in your daily work. He didn't create our lifespans for us to work harder, but to love Him more. As you journal your plans, prayers, feelings, and fears, ask Him to enrich your moments together so that His Spirit in you overflows into the entirety of your day.

THE FIVE LOVE LANGUAGES:
Physical Touch

How does God show His love to us through physical touch? It's important to remember that although God is Spirit, He created our physical bodies, and therefore cares very much for our physical wellness. In fact, one reason He sent His Son Jesus to become human was to experience the limitations of time and flesh, and to bring us physical healing. "And the people all tried to touch him, because power was coming from him and healing them all" (Luke 6:19). Yet evidence of God touching His people can be seen in the Old Testament, too. Perhaps the most stirring example of this can be found in Daniel 10, when Daniel had a vision of God meeting him in the form of a man:

Then I heard Him speaking, and as I listened to him, I fell into a deep sleep, my face to the ground. A hand touched me and set me trembling on my hands and knees. He said, "Daniel, you who are highly esteemed, consider carefully the words I am about to speak to you, and stand up, for I have now been sent to you." And when he said this to me, I stood up trembling. Then He continued, "Do not be afraid, Daniel. Since the first day that you set your mind to gain understanding and to humble yourself before your God, your words were heard, and I have come in response to them [...]" While he was saying this to me, I bowed with my face toward the ground and was speechless. Then one who looked like a man touched my lips, and I opened my mouth and began to speak. I said to the one standing before me, "I am overcome with anguish because of the vision, my lord, and I feel very weak. How can I, your servant, talk with you, my lord? My strength is gone and I can hardly breathe." Again the one who looked like a man touched me and gave me strength. "Do not be afraid, you who are highly esteemed," he said. "Peace! Be strong now; be strong." When he spoke to me, I was strengthened and said, "Speak, my lord, since you have given me strength. (Daniel 10:9-12, 15-19)

What a beautiful, inspiring picture of the awesome and compassionate God we serve! Through Jesus' physical death on the cross, we can claim Isaiah 53:5, "He was pierced for our transgressions, He was crushed for our iniquities; the punishment that brought us peace was on Him, and by His wounds we are healed." Yet His healing touch is always relational in context and includes emotional and spiritual sustenance, just like it was for Daniel. It is a heavenly language of love.

In addition to His healing touch, God's design for our physical wellness includes His provision of physical care within our relationships. He delights in bringing us together with others! Though physical intimacy in marriage is the most powerful example of this, the tender touch of friends and family can be an equally supportive gift from His hand.

Regarding marriage, Ephesians 5:28-31 describes it as a direct physical manifestation of Christ's relationship to us: "Husbands ought to love their wives as their own bodies. He who loves his wife loves himself. After all, no one ever hated their own body, but they feed and care for their body, just as Christ does the Church – for we are members of His body. For this reason a man will leave his father and mother and be united to his wife, and the two will become one flesh." For an even more detailed description of the kind of physical love that God envisions for marriage, check out Songs of Solomon. Its poetic, sensual images speak of a Creator who is masterful at overwhelming our physical senses when we follow his plan for marriage.

This isn't to say that singleness is not a valid calling from the Lord. I Corinthians 7 clearly says that it is. But all single women have moments when they ache for physical affection. So if you are single, and longing for the healing warmth of a hug or tender touch from a friend, ask God to bring another Christian woman into your life. When He does, speak with her openly and honestly about the physical loneliness you feel, and let her healing hands speak the love of Christ. As the Holy Spirit dwells inside each of us, there is power in laying our hands on each other in prayer. Not only does the warmth bring comfort and reassurance but imparts the power of God. The apostle Paul reminds Timothy in II Timothy 1:6 to "fan into flame the gift of God, which is in you through the laying on of my hands." After all, our physical bodies working together are what make us the Body of Christ.

So how do we offer physical touch as a language of worship to God? Jesus' coming to earth as a human was also the only time that we humans have been able to physically touch God directly, but only those whose touch was accompanied by faith received healing. Mark 5:24-34 tells the story of a woman who had been suffering from abnormal hemorrhaging for twelve years. Though the crowds pressed around Jesus continually, "she thought, 'If I just touch His clothes, I will be healed.' Immediately her bleeding stopped and she felt in her body that she was freed from her suffering. He said to her, 'Daughter, your faith has healed you.'" Jesus had been surrounded by a crowd of people all pressing against him, but this woman's touch was different. So now, even though we can't physically touch Jesus like we could when he walked the earth, we can still offer Him different physical symbols of the same faith this woman had, since it's faith that makes the difference.

One symbol is our bodily posture during worship. Notice the detailed mentioning of Daniel's postures when the Lord touched Him. He laid down prostrate. He trembled on his hands and knees. He stood up. He bowed with his face toward the ground. How might you use your body to symbolize the state of your heart during worship and prayer? Like the language of quality time, the language of physical touch can be used to help you more fully express your love for your Heavenly Father. Another way is to pretend to be a child in the presence of her adoring Daddy. Run, jump, dance, laugh, shout, raise your arms to the sky as a child would, stirring up the deep emotions you feel for God and allowing them to be released with heartfelt abandon. Women often have overwhelming emotions that we fight so hard to suppress and control. Yet by allowing them to be freely released to God in this way, we affirm to Him and to ourselves that both our faith and our feelings are important.

We also offer physical worship to God through choosing to dress modestly. Perhaps you've never thought about your clothing choices as having a spiritual basis, but they do. All women use their clothes to express their personalities and deeper parts of themselves, but as Christian women we have a responsibility to examine our motives and choose our clothing wisely. So perhaps it's time to think about what your clothes are communicating about you. We all want to look attractive, but we should be primarily dressing as a physical symbol of faith towards our loving Heavenly Father, letting Him shine His beauty through us. He knows the intents of our hearts, and He longs to be the One satisfying our emotional needs. So unlike other women who dress to demonstrate an *emptiness* needing to be filled, dress in a way that demonstrates a *fulfillment* for others to be attracted by. *Let others see you, not just notice what you have on.* Only then will they see the true inner beauty that comes from faith in Christ.

This week, open your mind and heart to new physical expressions of worship. Particularly if you are very reserved, let the exuberance of a child inspire you to dance, jump and extend your hands before your Abba Father. Or perhaps you need to kneel or lay prostrate before Him, as Daniel did in His presence. Then journal your feelings.

Plans and Prayers

In your journal, take the time to write down your plans and goals for the coming month of March.

What is your love language? How do you express it to God?

If Jesus were to return one year from today, what would you want to be found doing? What next step could you take to get there?

What prayer requests are on your heart this month? What answers and promises can you thank him for?

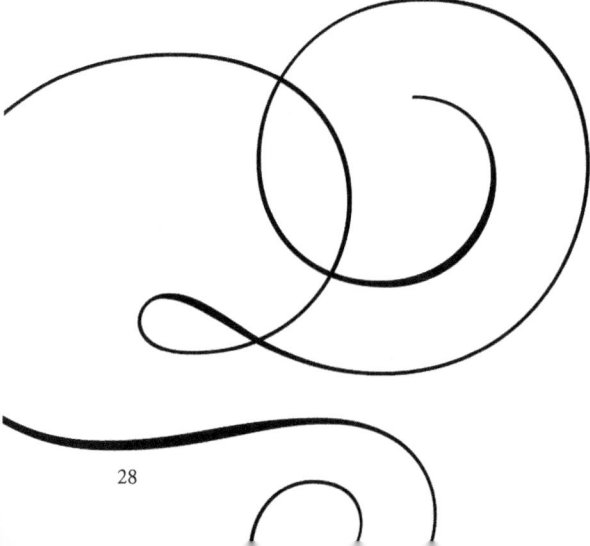

Feelings and Fears

What are you feeling today? Joyful? Burdened? Frustrated? Numb?

Does winter tend to get you down? How do you 'cope' with the dull moments of life?

Write out how you feel before God. He's been in your shoes and knows what you're going through.

What are you concerned about today? How might exploring a new love language of worship shift your gaze back to God in this area?

Freely journal about whatever comes to mind, as an act of surrendering it to Him.

March

The Five Love Languages:
Gifts

Gifts are as much a reflection of the giver as the receiver. They bestow honour on and reveal the character of both, bringing pleasure to each. God's gifts to us are more than just tokens of His love; they reveal to us more about Himself. We admire God's beauty through the gift of His creation around us and we seek to understand more of the gift of His image within us. We also have the gift of His Spirit, and spiritual gifts for use in our ministry to others.

A great way to start receiving God's gifts is by observing His creation. Romans 1:20 says, "for since the creation of the world God's invisible qualities – his eternal power and divine nature – have been clearly seen, being understood from what has been made." Therefore we can receive the gift of His creation by seeing His character in the natural world around us. There are profound aspects of God that can be appreciated by observing its beauty, and reading Psalm 104 is a great way to help bring this renewed perspective. From the majestic, strong mountain peaks to the fragile loveliness of a flower in bloom, we are given the gift of enjoying our awesome God who is both beautiful and strong!

Being made in the image of God is a gift we rarely think about, yet when we begin to unwrap all that sets us apart from other species we find greater purpose and blessing for our lives. Evolutionary theories have so penetrated society today that now both animals and humans are being esteemed and discarded at will, as if they had equal value. Human abortion and starvation are being permitted while animal cruelty is given the headlines. There's nothing wrong with being concerned about vulnerable animals, but we need to recognize how the unique gift of God's image in humanity is rarely accepted, let alone opened. As Christians, by viewing our human ability to speak, reason, create and emote as His Image in us, we proclaim our love for our Creator and affirm to the rest of humanity our distinct value in His eyes. May we recognize this amazing gift God has given to us and delve into it like a kid on Christmas morning!

The gift that further distinguishes Christians from other humans is the gift of the Holy Spirit. Through His Spirit, we have the privilege of direct communion with God so that He might display more of Himself, His character and His purposes. The gifts of character must be received first, and they are "love, joy, peace, patience, kindness, goodness, faithfulness, gentleness and self-control" (Galatians 5:22). Only when our characters begin to mature and grow will the specific purposes He has gifted us for begin to bloom. Romans 12:6-8 says, "We have different gifts, according to the grace given to each of us. If your gift is prophesying, then prophesy in accordance with your faith; if it is serving, then serve; if it is teaching, then teach; if it is to encourage, then give encouragement; if it is giving, then give generously; if it is to lead, do it diligently; if it is to show mercy, do it cheerfully." This is by no means an exhaustive list, but gives us a sample of the kinds of unique gifts the Spirit gives. The point is this: "to each one the manifestation of the Spirit is given for the common good" (1 Cor. 12:7).

We can never out-give God. All the gifts we have to offer He has given to us first. Yet He still delights in them as a language of our worship. Remember when you were a child and you asked your dad for some money so you could buy him a birthday present? Our hearts were generous but we knew our need, and we weren't too proud to ask. God doesn't mind when we ask in order to give; he designed us that way. He gave us dreams, abilities, and talents as children long before we could understand their developed purpose, so that we would delight in the life He gave us and boldly ask for more.

It's been said that our talents are God's gift to us, but how we use them is our gift to Him. Jesus told a parable about the wise stewardship of gifts in Matthew 25:14-30. He was speaking about the end times and describing the different ways that we will be evaluated on how we lived our lives. In the story, one man was given five talents by the master, and "went out at once and invested them and earned five more" (Matt. 25:16, ISV). A second man was given two, and likewise gained two more. However a third man was given one talent, and proceeded to dig a hole in the ground and buried it, because he was afraid. What buried talents might you have that you are afraid to bring to light? As children, we had such grand dreams of adventure, purpose and heroic feats, yet by our late teens we began to feel the enormous pressure from society to train for a sensible career in order to support ourselves. The key word is sensible – in the same way that burying money in the ground is sensible. Adults who don't like risk are afraid of losing what they have, since they lack a true understanding of the God they serve. Those who entirely serve Sensibility separate themselves from their own hearts, and from the heart of God. Yet what if those dreams and imagined feats of your childhood actually held the key to unlocking the truth about who you were really created to be? God places certain talents and gifts in our lives in order for us to develop them and live them out as our gift to Him; only then will we know true purpose and fulfillment as adults. Remember, gift-giving offers mutual honour and pleasure, and reveals characteristics of both the giver and the receiver. And this is particularly true in the gifts we give to God, because they came from Him anyway! Whoever said that re-gifting was wrong?

So, think of living out your unique calling as your supreme gift to God. He has designed a beautiful purpose for you and a potential that He is inviting you to step into: your own niche, if you like. To quote Frederick Buechner, it will be the place where your deepest fulfillment and the world's deepest need meet; where you find the greatest pleasure in doing the greatest good. For "each of you should use whatever gift you have received to serve others, as faithful stewards of God's grace in its various forms" (1 Peter 4:10). And it's never too late, because it's a place that's ready and waiting for you. If you're already there, it's always okay to ask for more.

This week, read and write out the Fruits of the Spirit in Galatians 5:22, and reflect on each one. As you spend time in worship, receive each one by name as a gift from God. Then reflect on your unique talents, passions and calling. Do you love to encourage other people? Serve behind the scenes? Teach from God's Word? Is God calling you to explore new opportunities to use the gifts He's given you? Step out in faith towards what you feel drawn to; the Spirit is calling you to experience greater purpose and pleasure for His glory. After all, mutual satisfaction is what gifts are all about.

The Five Love Languages:
Acts of Service

Of all the languages through which God has shown us His love, the greatest of all was His sacrificial sending of His Son. It was this ultimate act of service that paid the price for humanity's sin, and it cost Him a great deal, but His love for us made it worth it. He freely chose to expose His own Son to ridicule, misunderstanding, judgement, and execution in order that we may know His love and be free. John 3:16 is a favourite verse for many: "For God so loved the world that he gave his one and only Son, that whoever believes in him shall not perish but have eternal life." If that verse has become too familiar to you and has lost its poignancy, here's a lesser known one: "Since the children have flesh and blood, he too shared in their humanity so that by his death he might break the power of him who holds the power of death – that is, the devil – and free those who all their lives were held in slavery by their fear of death" (Hebrews 2:14-15). Jesus' sacrifice of Himself was painful and messy, but because of the joy set before Him He endured the cross and its shame, breaking death's hold on us and giving us eternal life. Acts of service differ from gifts by the magnitude of the prize that follows. For Jesus "made Himself nothing by taking the very nature of a servant, being made in human likeness. And being found in appearance as a man, He humbled Himself by becoming obedient to death – even death on a cross! Therefore God exalted Him to the highest place and gave Him the name that is above every name, that at the name of Jesus every knee should bow, in heaven and on earth and under the earth, and every tongue acknowledge that Jesus Christ is Lord, to the glory of God the Father" (Philippians 2:7-11). Of all the wonderful words of wisdom and works of healing Jesus offered during His life, it was the obedience He showed through His death that has made the greatest impact on humanity. The greater pain yielded a greater outcome. Being obedient is far more important to God than being talented; being honest greater than being generous. By humbling Himself, Jesus was exalted by God. Likewise when we humble ourselves, God will lift us up. In other words, if it's a question of developing either our character or gifting, God will choose character every time.

Acts of service can be painful, messy or simply inconvenient. They drain our resources and restrict our control of the outcome. They make us, well, servants! Yet Jesus said plainly, "the greatest among you will be your servant" (Matt. 23:11). Jesus himself, before He was crucified, demonstrated servanthood by washing His disciple's feet. Then He said to them, "now that I, your Lord and Teacher, have washed your feet, you also should wash one another's feet. I have set you an example that you should do as I have done for you. Very truly I tell you, no servant is greater than his master, nor is a messenger greater than the one who sent him" (John 13:14-16). So, if our Lord and Master gave us an example of servanthood to follow and instructed us to follow it, then we should obey Him in love, whether it's part of our gifting or not. After all, no act of service on our part could come close to His act of service for us.

Yet not too many of us like to obey. We like to feel in control, be the master, and give commands to someone else as our servant. That's why the most difficult love language for us to express to God is acts of service. As we've said, acts of service can be painful, messy or just plain inconvenient. They drain our resources and restrict our control of the outcome. They call us to draw from deep within our character, often thanklessly, rather than our areas of talent. Acts of service exercise our humility and cut down our pride. Yet because of the sacrifice they require, they yield the most enduring good.

But like all other languages of worship we've discussed, our acts of service to God must primarily come from right motives: a heart overflowing with love for a Savior who sacrificed more for us than we could ever offer Him in return. We also need to act in faith, trusting that He will fill us up with even greater abundance as we deplete ourselves in His service. So when you see a need, are you quick to step in and help, with no questions asked or strings attached, regardless of whose job you think it is or who gets the credit? Or do you hesitate, feeling unqualified or unavailable? By responding to these invitations to serve, we can offer a language of worship that will profoundly touch the heart of God – particularly when we choose to serve the people He values the most.

Firstly, God loves Jewish people. Jesus came to earth as a Jew, and the good news He preached about the coming Kingdom of God was given to them first. Paul writes in Romans 1:16, "For I am not ashamed of the gospel, because it is the power of God that brings salvation to everyone who believes: first to the Jew, then to the Gentile." Jews have been severely mistreated, tortured, ridiculed and passionately hated throughout history, yet numerous attempts at extermination have not removed them from the earth or from God's heart. By choosing to find ways to serve Jewish people, you are choosing to minister directly to the heartbeat of God. When God first established His chosen people through Abraham, he promised him, "I will bless those who bless you, and whoever curses you I will curse; and all peoples on earth will be blessed through you" (Gen. 12:3). God promises us in His Word that He will pour out blessing on those who serve, protect, defend and minister to the Jews. Even making a sacrifice of time to pray for them and for the land of Israel can bring significant eternal impact and touch God's heart.

Secondly, God loves orphaned, widowed, destitute, defenseless people. People who have lost all means of supporting themselves or their families and have no voice to bring change. Though we are certainly aware of this need in the third world, providing for orphans and widows in our Western context means defending the rights of the unborn, supporting single mothers, and combatting human trafficking. Proverbs 31:8-9 says, "Speak up for those who cannot speak for themselves, for the rights of all who are destitute. Speak up and judge fairly; defend the rights of the poor and needy." There are vulnerable people in Africa, on the next street over, and in the womb. By choosing to pray for and give to such as these that the Lord lays on your heart, your service will deeply touch His heart in return.

Thirdly, God loves His Church. Galatians 6:10 says, "Therefore, as we have opportunity, let us do good to all people, especially to those who belong to the family of believers." He is the Bridegroom, and we are the bride. He loves when we unite together and serve each other, for in so doing we are serving Him. We all know the unique trials and struggles that come with being a Christian in this evil world, so by sacrificially serving other Christians, we edify God's Church, further His purposes, and touch His heart. May your acts of service flow from a heart overcome by His love and satisfy the needs of the people He cares for the most.

This week, examine your heart for areas of pride or reluctance to serve outside of your gifting. Jesus didn't wash the disciples' filthy feet because he was the best foot-washer in Palestine, but because it needed doing and it communicated the Father's heart in a powerful way. Reflect on how you might communicate and bless the Father's heart by serving these three people groups more intentionally. Blessing the Father's heart is the heart of worship.

THE FIVE LOVE LANGUAGES:
Practicing a Worship Spectrum

In order to bring together all we've discussed about the Five Love Languages of Worship, I thought I would highlight several ways our relationship to God is symbolized in the Bible and how these symbols build in intensity. As different circumstances in our lives dictate which form we identify with most at a given time, so will our language of worship expression change. You may even choose to use these different physical postures to symbolize each relationship within your own worship lifestyle.

- Potter & clay – "We are the clay, you are the Potter; we are all the work of your hand" (Isaiah 64:8). The Potter can form, deform, and reform the clay according to His good pleasure. As clay, we can picture our physical bodies as dry, cracked and decaying, yet we are still the created objects of the Potter. With the Holy Spirit inside these earthen vessels, our cracks and holes simply allow His light to shine through that much brighter. When we feel broken, fragile, or lifeless, we can worship our Potter with open, extended hands, offering our emptiness and our desire to be molded and filled for His purposes.

- Shepherd & sheep – "For you were like sheep going astray,

but now you have returned to the Shepherd and Overseer of your souls" (1 Peter 2:25). As sheep, we hover close to the ground looking for food, often wandering aimlessly without perspective. We require our Shepherd's watchful eye to protect us, keep us together, and lead us in paths of righteousness. Though the Shepherd guards and cares for the sheep, so also the Shepherd can sacrifice the sheep on the altar as He wishes. Yet Jesus came as the Lamb of God to pay the sacrifice we each deserved. When we feel lost, scared, or alone, we can kneel in worship to better remind ourselves of a sheep's perspective in relation to the Shepherd, and yield our fears and desires to the one who can see the big picture.

- Master & servant – "No servant is greater than his master, nor is a messenger greater than the one who sent him. Now that you know these things, you will be blessed if you do them" (John 13:16-17). The saints of the Bible often referred to themselves as bondservants of Christ. They had no plans or desires of their own, but purely worked toward the will of their Master. Slavery was an economic reality in those days, but it wasn't necessarily a bad role, providing you had a kind and honest master. In Jesus, we have the best - he has given us all we need to obey His commands and follow His example without question. When we sin, or feel tempted to abandon our responsibilities, we can lie prostrate in worship, as a sign of repentance and homage to the Master. There is something about worshipping prostrate that dispels pride and develops reverence in a heart that we must recognize is not our own.

- Father & child – "The Spirit himself testifies with our spirit that we are God's children. Now if we are children, then we are heirs – heirs of God and co-heirs with Christ, if indeed we share in his sufferings in order that we may also share in his glory" (Romans 8:16-17). Like servants, children have no real rights or freedom of their own, yet there is a difference.

Children have identity and hope of inheritance. Though they must obey and endure discipline now, they have relational kinship with their Father and a claim to inheriting all He has. When you feel unsure of yourself or unappreciated, reach your hands up to your heavenly Father in worship as a young girl would to her daddy. When you feel happy and carefree, laugh, run, dance, and jump before the One who delights in you as His daughter. Through our brother Jesus, He longs to pour the riches of His grace into your heart.

- Friend & friend – "I no longer call you servants, because a servant does not know his master's business. Instead I have called you friends, for everything that I learned from my Father I have made known to you" (John 15:15). Friends share a relational intimacy and mutual understanding that is the result of personal choice. Servants are chosen, too, but for what they can do. Friends are chosen for who they are. What characteristics do you value in your closest friends? I am deeply honoured when a friend stops what they are doing, becomes still, and listens to what I have to say. Sharing secrets, deep fears, and cherished dreams are some of the exciting exchanges that can take place in those moments of stillness. So when you feel worried, stressed, or too busy, take the time to be still and have a heart-to-heart talk with your best Friend. The physical discipline of stopping, being still and listening to the Lord can remind us of the intimate bond of friendship that He has chosen us to share with Him.

- Groom & bride – "I promised you as a pure bride to one husband – Christ" (2 Corinthians 11:2, NLT). This verse brings us full circle: our Potter, who formed us out of the dust of the ground, has now raised us up to the most intimate and honoured position of a bride to His Son, the Bridegroom. Chosen as one chooses a friend, but now united in a way that is much more intimate and binding. The bride is given identity, intimacy, status, and glory by her Bridegroom, who has laid down His life so He can be with her. I don't know about you, but I feel unworthy of such an honour. Yet we can posture ourselves as His bride by meditating on what is pure and wholesome, so that our Bridegroom will continue to rejoice over us in greater and greater measure. We can also dress modestly and practice chastity, guarding our hearts and bodies, remembering that this most intimate of human relationships was designed to be the closest reflection of God's relationship with us.

I hope you've enjoyed this Love Language series – I've certainly enjoyed writing it. I pray you are inspired to look for unique expressions of worship that reflect where you are on the worship spectrum. It is not a ladder to be climbed, but rather a piano to be played as your heart's melody changes throughout life. Simply rest in the fact that you can offer your Potter, Shepherd, Master, Father, Friend, and Groom different worship languages, rooted in the Spirit and in Truth, that most aptly reflect your heart's motions of emotion each day.

FOR HIS NAME'S SAKE:
REFLECTIONS ON PSALM 23

Several years ago, I came across the book *A Shepherd Looks at Psalm 23* by Phillip Keller. In it, Keller sheds profound insight into one of the most familiar psalms ever written through having made his living for several years as a shepherd in East Africa. Like the psalmist David, Keller understands all that it means to be a sheep, and to have the Lord as his shepherd. The Hebrew word for 'shepherd' means feeder, provider, keeper, protector, gatherer, and friend to the sheep. Keller observes that a good shepherd must make endless sacrifices for the welfare of his sheep, since sheep require more attention than any other class of livestock. Yet when managed correctly, they can be of great benefit to the land and to mankind.

In the original Hebrew, Psalm 23 reads as a chiastic poem, where each line points to the central phrase "for His name's sake" (Psalm 23:3c). A person's name carries a lot with it – their reputation, character, status, who they're related to, and more. The more we study God's Word, the more we learn all that His great Name carries, and the richer our worship of Him becomes. For not only do we see his invisible attributes in the created world around us, but the Bible tells the narrative of His *character* revealed through the stories of His relations with humanity. Often when God revealed something new about himself to a person in the Bible, they give him a new name. These have come to be known as the Redemptive Names of God, which are each echoed in Psalm 23. In other words, David wrote this psalm in order to clearly emphasize that the Lord our shepherd, *Jehovah Raha*, has such diligence and care for us because *his reputation is at stake*. Throughout Scripture God reveals to us that shepherding is not just what He does, *it's who He is*. He feels the full weight of responsibility for rescuing and sustaining his people - even to the point of sending His own Son to die for us - so that we can rest in the guarantee that His Name carries.

As our shepherd, God is also *Jehovah Jireh*, who provides for our needs. This is celebrated in the phrase "I shall not want". As we all know, there is a difference between wanting and needing; between what we feel we deserve and what is best for us. At the highest level, God supplies all our needs (Philippians 4:19). We can be assured that this is never up for discussion. It is part of who He is to us. Yes, suffering and injustice still exist, but we must trust God to redeem these situations and use them to shape our hearts. God is first addressed as *Jehovah Jireh* in Genesis 22:14 when God provided a ram for Abraham to use as a sacrifice instead of his son Isaac. Only after Abraham had fully demonstrated his trust in God's sovereign will was the need for a sacrifice met. In other words, being free from want requires being filled with trust.

As our shepherd, God is *Jehovah Shalom*, who is our peace. He "makes me lie down in green pastures" and "leads me beside still waters". Keller observes that sheep will only lie down if they are free from fear, conflict, parasites, hunger, *or if the shepherd is with them*. Yes, our shepherd provides for our needs, leading us to rest in the peace that it brings, but peace is also possible in the midst of the storm when we learn that *His very presence is our peace*. Gideon was the first to recognize this in Judges 6:22-24. "When Gideon realized that it was the angel of the LORD, he exclaimed, "Alas, Sovereign LORD! I have seen the angel of the LORD face to face! But the LORD said to him, "Peace! Do not be afraid. You are not going to die." So Gideon built an altar to the LORD there and called it 'The LORD is Peace'." Gideon was a classic anxious sheep. Yet once he received this revelation, the Spirit of God literally 'clothed himself with Gideon' (Judges 6:34) and used him to win a mighty victory. At the end of the day, His presence is all that mattered.

As our shepherd, God is *Jehovah Rapha*, who "restores my soul". Keller recounts how sheep, either lazy or heavy with wool, often get turned on their backs and are unable to right themselves. Vulnerable to attack or starvation, these sheep would die unless the shepherd 'restored' them to their feet. God reveals this about Himself to Israel in Exodus 15:26, after leading them across the Red Sea. "If you listen carefully to the LORD your God and do what is right in his eyes, if you pay attention to his commands and keep all his decrees, I will not bring on you any of the diseases I brought on the Egyptians, for I am the LORD, who heals you." Regardless of how we get 'upturned' in life, God delights in healing and restoring us – it's in His name and who He is.

As our shepherd, God is *Jehovah Tsidkinu*, who "leads me in paths of righteousness". Sheep are creatures of habit, continually grazing in the same place or going astray, observes Keller. They need to be constantly moved and led by the shepherd to new pastures. David's words here in Psalm 23 begin to be prophetic, foreshadowing Jeremiah 23:5-6: "'The days are coming,' declares the LORD, when I will raise up for David a righteous Branch, a King who will reign wisely and do what is just and right in the land. In his days Judah will be saved and Israel will live in safety. This is the name by which he will be called: The LORD our Righteous Savior." Yet to be led in paths of righteousness, we need to learn to follow. Having now built up a trust in his presence and power to heal and provide, we must now make a *conscious choice to obey*. This is the difference between name-only Christians and those who actually follow Christ. Once we understand how our righteousness is like filthy rags to His, we can choose to follow Him for His righteous name's sake.

At this point in Psalm 23, we reach the central axis and theme, and the language becomes more direct. No longer does the sheep speak *about* the shepherd, but now *to* Him. "Even though I walk through the valley of the shadow of death, I will fear no evil, for *You are with me*." Our shepherd is *Jehovah Shammah*, 'the Lord is there'. This name is equivalent to Emmanuel, 'God with us'. The sending of both Jesus and the Holy Spirit demonstrates the lengths God will go to dwell with us and in us. As sheep are led to new pastures and higher ground, Keller describes how the best route is often filled with valleys and shadows, because it's the only place along the way where ample food and water can be found. Yes, there are storms, predators, and darkness, but with the shepherd we are free from fear and isolation.

As our shepherd, God is *Jehovah Nissi*, "The Lord is my banner". He prepares a table before me in the presence of my enemies. As our banner, God goes before us in battle, fighting and preparing the way for us. We stand under his protective covering and look up to Him for our strength. Moses was the first to call God his banner in Exodus 17:15, when Israel was given victory over the Amalekites. Keller would add that after sheep are led through the valleys, they finally arrive at the high mountain 'tables' where they feed over the summer. Shepherds take great diligence to prepare this pasture before the sheep arrive and keep watch over their flock day and night. This reminds me of the shepherds who kept watch over their flocks the night Jesus was born. Because of their diligence and care for their sheep, they were given the honor of being the first to meet the Shepherd of their souls!

In Ezekiel 34, we find a beautiful example of God describing himself as Israel's shepherd, which now includes you and me through Jesus. As you read the following passage, reflect on the traits of a shepherd just described. "This is what the Sovereign Lord says: I myself will search for my sheep and look after them. As a shepherd looks after his scattered flock when he is with them, so will I look after my sheep. I will rescue them from all the places where they were scattered on a day of clouds and darkness. I will bring them out from the nations and gather them from the countries, and I will bring them into their own land. I will pasture them on the mountains of Israel, in the ravines and in all the settlements in the land. I will tend them in a good pasture, and the mountain heights of Israel will be their grazing land. There they will lie down in good grazing land, and there they will feed in a rich pasture on the mountains of Israel" (Ezekiel 34:11-14). Can you identify with being a sheep? If so, let God be your guiding shepherd – on the mountains and in the valleys, in fear or in rest. He promises to come through. His very name depends on it.

This week, meditate on these Redemptive names of God in the context of Psalm 23. How do they enhance your worship? Journal freely about your sheep-like tendencies and how you could better trust and obey Him because of His name and all that it stands for.

Midwives of the Soul

Life coaching is one of the fastest-growing career fields of our day, primarily because it helps people navigate and sustain positive changes in their lives. I was drawn to coaching for several reasons, primarily because I wanted to experience the abundant life Jesus promised and I wanted to help other women find the same. Having a life coach is particularly helpful during emotionally dry seasons or when one is contemplating major life change. The listening ear and supportive friendship a coach offers does much to minimize feelings of fear and isolation that often accompany moving forward into something new. In short, a life coach is a lot like a midwife of the soul.

Women have been giving birth for thousands of years, but each is a beautifully new experience because each mother, child, and practitioner is different. So it is with coaching. God has placed inside each of us dreams and potential realities that often require the affirmation and encouragement from others to bring to life. The term 'midwife' derives from the old English terms *mid* meaning 'with' and *wif* meaning 'woman' – someone who was with a woman during childbirth.

We all have critical seasons in our lives when we feel it is more painful to stay where we are than to step into the unknown, but simply moving away from pain is usually not enough to get us to where we ought to be – we also need passion. Only by being drawn *towards* something passionately will we ultimately find fulfillment and realize our potential.

The Bible offers us two stories of midwives and the power they had to shift situations. In Exodus 1, the King of Egypt said to the Hebrew midwives, Shiphrah and Puah, "When you are helping the Hebrew women during childbirth on the delivery stool, if you see that the baby is a boy, kill him, but if it is a girl, let her live." The midwives, however, feared God and did *not* do what the King of Egypt ordered them to do. They let the boys live. So God was kind to the midwives and gave them families of their own. Midwives must be very courageous and maintain their faith in dire and difficult circumstances. When the pain of labour is strongest, or the draw of passion dwindles for a moment, the midwife is needed to carry that passion and call it forth on the mother's behalf.

In Genesis 38, we find Tamar in labour with twin boys. As one boy put out a hand, the midwife tied it with a scarlet thread. But amazingly he drew back his hand, and his brother came out first! So the midwife declared, "What a breakthrough (*parats*) you have made for yourself!" So he was named Perez, and he is found in the lineage of Jesus in Matthew 1:3. The power of a midwife's words cannot be measured. When the mother is at her most vulnerable, the midwife offers clear perspective and profound insight that can carry great leverage.

In birthing a new vision, dream or change, coaches want to ensure that it is life-giving and fulfilling for the 'mom-to-be', lines up with her values, and is kept in balance with everything else. Just as midwives are careful to ensure both mother and baby are healthy and ready for the delivery, so coaches should offer discernment and direction to mothers when needed, ultimately inspiring them to take greater care of their own health and wellness. Those caught in addictions or harmful behaviours need counselling, not coaching, and should be referred accordingly.

Providing education and wellness instruction is one of the lesser-known roles a midwife or coach might fulfill. When done in a group setting, it provides great value to pre-moms, and it introduces the personality and character of the midwife or coach to their prospective clients. The learning may then continue individually, according to the particular needs of each mother.

With both midwives and coaches, establishing a strong relationship built on mutual trust is paramount. The power of the midwife coupled with the vulnerability of the mother in such an intimate and emotionally-charged environment demands it. The midwife invites the mother to welcome change and to view it positively; to push away from the pain and pull towards the passion. The midwife likely has been in her shoes; offering counsel and guidance when requested. The midwife challenges and questions limiting mindsets and perspectives, gently exhorting a higher view. No matter what, the midwife becomes a vital figure of support, comfort, and affirmation; a faithful and tender encourager and friend.

Once the new life has been birthed, the midwife can help the mother brainstorm and troubleshoot how best to manage and structure her new reality to ensure a smooth transition and to optimize growth. Through it all, she can offer spiritual wisdom to the mother on how to loosen her grasp, wiggle her fingers, and find enjoyment in the process. Pain and uncertainty never end, and life will always remain out of our control. Only faith in God and obedience to His commands will ensure we remain securely in His plan, and a wise midwife or coach knows how to communicate this to everyone she touches, inspiring that abundant life Jesus promises all who trust Him.

This week, reflect on the profound effect others have had on your life during seasons of crisis, transition, or uncertain change. Whether it was a hospital staff member, pastor, counsellor, or friend, the influence of others during times of heightened emotion leaves a lasting impression.

How have you been a midwife of the soul to someone else? Journal this week about how you felt during these times, both as a 'mother' and as a 'midwife', asking God to reveal to you how He saw you in those moments.

Plans and Prayers

In your journal, take the time to write down your plans and goals for the coming month of April.

What are some practical ways you can implement new expressions of worship into your life?

What does your name mean? As you reflect on Jesus' death and resurrection this Easter, pray that it would continue to reveal His powerful name and character across the world.

What prayer requests are on your heart this month? What answers and promises can you thank him for? What do you need to confess to him?

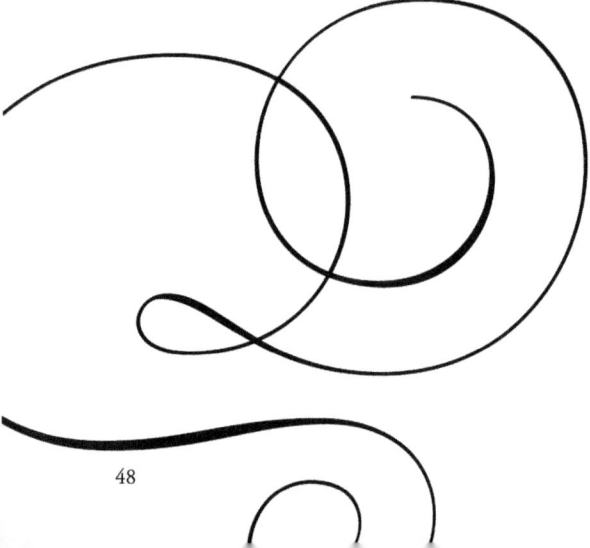

Feelings and Fears

What are you feeling today? Joyful? Burdened? Frustrated? Numb?

How are you responding to disappointment right now? How might a coach or counsellor help you take a higher view?

Write out how you feel before God. He's been in your shoes and knows what you're going through.

What is the downside of believing everything you think?

Freely journal about whatever comes to mind, as an act of surrendering it all to Him.

April

Scuba Faith

It's story time! I thought I would include this illustration as a creative way to bring the Christian faith journey alive for you. And guess what! You get to play the starring role! Are you ready?

Picture yourself before accepting Jesus. You are living your life for yourself, going from one beach party high to the next. You have lots of friends and a glamorous career as a lifeguard, but deep down you feel unfulfilled. Then you meet someone dressed in scuba gear who tells you about how amazing life is under the water – and you accept Jesus at her invitation. You put on the scuba gear she gives you and begin reading the manual of the Bible on how all this stuff works. By taking up this new hobby you meet lots of other people who enjoy scuba diving near the shore on Sunday or even several times a week, and you learn a lot of the basics from them. You still hang out with your friends at the beach, but you feel different than you used to and don't really know why. You feel greater purpose and hope than you ever have before, and the open acceptance you receive from your new friends is wonderful, but there's no way you could ever see yourself keeping this suit on all the time. Yet soon you begin to see a few scuba divers who go a lot further out and stay down for days and days. They must have professional equipment and special training, you think. Too expensive for my budget. But how do they have enough oxygen for such a long time? Your curiosity has almost become unbearable when you finally spot a diver returning to the surface after being submerged for months. You are so curious you have to go up and ask. She begins to tell you stories of magnificent sea creatures and sunken treasures that you have to see to believe. "But what about the oxygen?" you ask. Oh, she explains, whenever the tank reaches empty, it miraculously fills up again. She does these long, deep dives so often, she no longer worries about the basic necessity to breathe. She has surrendered her all to God, committed to follow His agenda, and now lives to explore all He desires to show her, knowing He will supply all her needs. Her eyes are shining as she speaks and you can't help but believe that what she is saying is true, yet your logical mind still doubts the whole oxygen miracle thing. You still have questions, yet you are willing to give it a try. What do you have to lose? So down into the ocean you go, but this time farther out than you have before and for longer. Your oxygen is now almost gone, but instead of panicking you decide to pray and ask God to provide. Just at that moment you see the most beautifully-coloured school of fish swimming in the distance. Your heart melts as you are overwhelmed by God's amazing beauty and remember how much more valued you are than they, which are here one day, then food for a shark the next. As you swim over to take a closer look, you discover that your oxygen tank is full! How did that happen? It's against the laws of nature! Then you hear inside your heart the Lord say, "I created the laws of nature, and I created you. I love you. This is what I have created you for. Come deeper with me and I will show you even greater things than these." By now you no longer feel any resistance or desire to question, only willing obedience. As you penetrate deeper and deeper into unknown waters, your spirit expands with every new discovery, and you know your heart has found its true fulfillment. The adventure, the wonder, and the mystery that is being unveiled before your very eyes causes you to see even yourself in a different light. You think, "If the Creator of all this beauty cares enough about me to sustain my physical needs, pursue my heart, and speak so intimately with me, I must have some value, and something of value to give in return." The picture starts to become clear. It's only now you begin to feel an incredible urge to return to the surface, but not for air. Your heart is filling with compassion for those friends you left on the beach. If only they could be here experiencing this, too! You begin to wonder how you will explain it to them. What will you say? How can you even put into words all the amazing things you've witnessed and discovered, let alone explain to them how the whole oxygen miracle works? Still, you have learned very well by now the deep thrills that follow obedience, so you slowly rise to the surface, confident that the Lord will be with you and will put His words in your mouth, as even now He puts oxygen in your lungs.

Called to Creativity

The story of creation in Genesis 1 is an incredibly powerful passage, and profoundly meaningful. In it, we see God speaking invisible words that bring a visible world into being. (That fact alone should bring greater increase to our faith!) He is pleased with what He has made, but we sense a momentum building when God describes His creating *us*. Genesis 1:27 says, "So God created mankind in his own image, in the image of God he created them; male and female he created them." Notice how the same phrase is said three times in three different ways? This parallelism is used for emphasis so that we as humans, and particularly as women, know the importance of the divine image we possess. Doesn't it make sense, therefore, that one way we can know more about God is by discovering and living out His image in us? Since the Fall in Genesis 3, this Image has been tainted, calloused, and buried, so it's no wonder that we struggle with living lives of true purpose and fulfillment. Yet Creator God is also Redeemer God, and He longs to purify, restore, and reveal His unique reflection in you.

So how can we best facilitate the recovery of this invisible, multifaceted jewel within the decaying mess of our lives? The key is creativity. God has given each of us the potential to create, enrich, inspire, and influence. Just as God used intangible words to produce a world of enduring beauty, likewise He created us to deposit a part of ourselves into everything we create, and to bring us pleasure and fulfillment from it. What an incredible gift we've been given from the God who created us! Imagine how much pleasure you give your Creator just by being His daughter! We bear His image, and we have been given the opportunity to glorify Him by creating in return. So, ask Him to reveal more of His creative attributes and purposes to your heart as a way of honouring Him and respecting His image that you bear. What an amazing privilege!

How are you creative? If nothing comes to mind right away, just remember that we all function and think differently. Even if you don't consider yourself to be artistic, take a moment to think outside the conventional creative arts. Are you a good problem solver or manager? Do you dream of new inventions that would make the world better? Do you like to cook? Work with children? Are you a people person who loves to make new friends to both inspire and learn from? As God brings things to mind, consider taking a risk and try something new. Remember, the key to true fulfillment is finding the point where your deepest passion and the world's deepest need meet.

Perhaps you've been struggling with feelings of low self-worth that are preventing you from reaching out of yourself. Believe that God has given you unique gifts of self-expression He has designed for His purposes, and He wants you to live them out so He can bless you! They are part of who He created you to be as His precious daughter and the one who carries His stamp of workmanship. Begin to pray and ask Him to open the door of creative expression in your heart, and then step out in faith.

Perhaps you are a very talented woman in many areas, always ready and willing to give of yourself, but often feel burnt out. This is a problem that many women struggle with. There always seems to be so much to do and so little time in which to do it. Keep in mind the model God used in creating the world: He chose what to create, brought it into being with great focus and purpose, admired and blessed what He had made, and then *He rested*. Busy women particularly need to practice saying 'no' to some things so they may approach their life's work with focused energy and purpose, and then allow themselves to take pleasure in it and rest from it.

We also must remember that creativity often involves suffering and struggle. Some of the world's most innovative solutions and creative ideas came forth during the darkest days of World War II. The enemy was real, resources were limited, and people bonded together. In fact, many who lived during that time described those years as the best of their lives. Though evil was all around, when they clung to hope and to each other, they found unity, innovation, and purpose cultivated. The will to live is a powerful thing.

And yet, there is a battle going on in the spiritual realm right now. A war has been declared against your heart, your family, the Church, and the whole Image-bearing human race, and eternity is at stake. Perhaps you've even been wounded in the battle. God is with you right now, longing to bind up your wounds and help you to step out and fight in the unique and creative way He has given you, despite the pain. He has already sent His Son Jesus to earth as the ultimate sacrificial offering, to pay the price for your healing and salvation. Though the struggle continues, the Victor in this war has already been decided. Will you accept the victorious life He offers so you can live as a war hero rather than a prisoner? The greatest heroes are those who have been prisoners; their tenacity of spirit is more courageous, contagious, and compassionate because of their former brokenness and despair. So, what good things do you want to create, particularly out of your suffering? What specific danger or painful circumstance is inspiring you to fight for the values you hold dear? God is speaking to each one of us about our different areas of creativity that can bring great personal fulfillment and healing to ourselves and to our world, all while the war continues to rage around us. The end is near, when God will restore His creation once again to a state of beauty and wholeness. He calls us now to foretell His coming through displaying His creative power to a world in need.

This week, consider your life's struggles from a different perspective. How might God be using your pain to bring forth beauty? What mindsets need to shift so that you no longer see yourself as a prisoner of war, but a war hero? Journal freely what comes to mind and include some creative ways you might cultivate this new mindset in others. If you tend to get burnt out, journal some meaningful activities that would bring more rest to your routine and more time to enjoy the work of your hands.

CREATIONAL RHYTHM

Do you like routine? Some people find repetition boring and monotonous; others find it comforting and reassuring. Wherever you stand, we serve a God of both constancy and newness. Think about it: does the coming of spring each year fill you with boredom or with wonder? How about the first snowfall? After each day of creation in the book of Genesis, God saw what He had made, and declared it good. And now, thousands of years later, God still delights in repeating the same ebb and flow of the seasons as if they were the pulsating rhythm to His favourite song.

In contrast, we humans tend to seek after adventure, excitement, or any distraction to break the apparent monotony of our lives. We are a restless species, striving for wealth, position, and greater power. The passing of each year only reminds us that we're getting older, and we grimace at the prospect of greater pain and fatigue and lesser beauty and dignity. Unlike the rest of creation, we know we will face death someday, and recoil from what time does to us. We wear ourselves out trying to make the most of our youth rather than embracing each day as it comes, and we forget that having 'eternity in our hearts' was meant to inspire hope and not dread.

Yet what does the Bible say? "Though outwardly we are wasting away, yet inwardly we are being renewed day by day. For our light and momentary troubles are achieving for us an eternal glory that far outweighs them all" (2 Corinthians 4:16-17). When you look in the mirror, your first thought may not be "God, your creation is good!" but rest assured, you can be confident that your spiritual beauty increases every day you embrace His timing. This is the dynamic nature of God's creational rhythm. Like ascending a spiral staircase, you may feel as though you're going in repetitive circles, but He is also leading you higher.

The garden is one of the most life-giving places for me to be. Whether it's my own or someone else's, formal or wild, floral or herbal, gardens nurture my soul. A friend once observed this and spoke Isaiah 58:11 over my life. It has since become my life verse: "The Lord will guide you always; he will satisfy your needs in a sun-scorched land and will strengthen your frame. You will be like a well-watered garden, like a spring whose waters never fail." I even created a painting of this verse, which depicts an elegant bench situated beside a bubbling brook within a lovely green formal garden. Just outside the garden's gate, however, is a vast desert wilderness of thorns and tumbleweeds parched by the searing sun. That's a lot like our souls when we're striving for excitement, power, and beauty outside of God's purposes, isn't it? But inside the garden's gate, we are invited to linger on the bench in the cool shade while the brook sings over us. Only through resting in God's timing and not resisting his creational rhythm will we experience this daily spiritual renewal promised to us. Like a garden, we too must experience seasons - rest and activity, pruning and growth, drought and abundance. So much more goes on under the ground than above it, and there's always something happening that we can't see. Roots go deeper during drought, and branches thicken during winter. God alone ordains how each season in your life will contribute to a fruitful harvest. He simply asks for your patience and to find the beauty inherent in each one. Isaiah 51:3 says, "The Lord will surely comfort Zion and will look with compassion on all her ruins; he will make her deserts like Eden, her wastelands like the garden of the Lord. Joy and gladness will be found in her, thanksgiving and the sound of singing." What a fabulous promise! Even sun-scorched desert lives can be restored into lush gardens by the redemptive hand of God, as beautifully as He brings about the coming of spring.

After all, the Garden of Eden was God's original setting for mankind, and a garden tomb the setting for Jesus' resurrection. John 20 recounts the story of that glorious Easter Sunday morning, where Mary Magdalene meets her risen Lord. Let's join her in this moment. She is standing outside the empty tomb crying, because she thinks his body has been taken. Just at that moment, a man approaches whom she believes is the gardener. Only after he says her name does she recognize that it is Jesus! "Teacher!" she cries, holding him in delight! Jesus had completely healed and delivered Mary from seven demons three years earlier, and her life had not been the same since. She learned from him, followed him and supported him even up to his death on a cross. In a culture where women were marginalized, Jesus' life and ministry were like a well-watered garden to her dry and ravaged soul. And so how fitting is it that she now believes him to be the gardener! He commissions her to go and tell the other disciples that he is alive, a glorious honour that we still carry to this day as his redemptive plan for creation continues to unfold before our eyes.

This Easter, reflect with wonder and gratitude on the price Jesus paid and the victory he won for you. No longer do we have to strive in our own strength, but simply receive the abundant life he offers – a life spent in the garden. Journal freely and honestly about how that makes you feel. Is it relieving? Frustrating? Painful at times? Take a deep breath, allowing his healing, living water to flood your soul. Allow both the natural coming of spring and the supernatural coming of Easter to remind you of the greatness of our God and cause you to trust His perfect creational rhythm.

Owning Versus Stewarding

How did it feel to buy your first home? I vividly remember the excitement of getting the keys from the lawyer's office, and then walking into that empty front hall that still smelled like fresh paint. I loved my first house, and it was such a thrill to personalize it, decorate it and make it my own. But over time, as you may know, the excitement fades and the reality of the time and cost involved in cleaning and maintaining the property takes over. You still love your house, but now part of that love becomes the permission you give yourself to be lazy and put things off. We have the freedom to clean and fix-up as much or as little of life as we want, and yet we often let things slide little by little, allowing more urgent demands and distractions to take priority.

But now let's consider the scenario of stewarding. I took a vacation recently, travelling to a nearby city. I knew people who lived there, and I was able to find friends who were willing to let me stay in their house. They were taking a vacation that same week, so the house was empty. I was essentially stewarding their property during my stay. How did my behaviour differ that week from living in my own home? I was extremely careful, diligent to clean up after myself, mindful to not waste electricity or water, and cautious when using their dishes and furniture lest I break or stain anything. They didn't ask me to be a careful steward, I simply felt such an inner sense of gratitude for their generosity that I wanted to honour them and their home.

Do you see the distinction between owning and stewarding? The owning mindset is all about individuality and free choice, whereas the stewarding mindset is about *relationship*. Yes, God gives us ownership and free choice, which we can use to our detriment. Yet only true fulfillment and purpose can be found when we recognize and choose to be *stewards* of our lives rather than *owners*.

Jesus tells a parable in Matthew 25:14-30 called the Parable of the Talents. A business owner was going on a journey, and so entrusted some of his wealth to three stewards according to their ability. Two of the stewards, wishing to honour the man, worked hard to make a profit on the investment entrusted to them. The third man, however, buried the money in the ground, stating that he was afraid of the owner. What do you think really happened? Was this steward simply lazy, hoping to get something for nothing? Or did he distrust and resent the owner? Either way, the problem was due to an incorrect mindset that was not centred on relationship. Clearly the owner already knew the limited ability of the third man, having given him the smallest share. (How often do you feel the unfairness of distribution?) You still have a choice, however. You can still choose to be a good steward of the little you have, honouring the Lord in gratitude, rather than comparing yourself to others or cultivating bitterness and distrust in your heart.

So, what are we called to steward?

- Our bodies and our health. I Corinthians 6:19-20 states, "Do you not know that your bodies are temples of the Holy Spirit, who is in you, whom you have received from God? You are not your own; you were bought at a price. Therefore honour God with your bodies." This is the key verse to understand with regards to stewarding. We are not our own. We were bought at a price, and now house the Holy Spirit inside us. His is the inner direction that we need to listen to and obey in this journey of stewardship. The Scriptures provide all the tools we need to perform this awesome task well and with the correct relational focus. So with this in mind, what do you need to do to achieve and maintain optimal health? What habits do you need to change? What foods and activities do you need to avoid? What does moderation and balance look like to you realistically?

- Our time. James 4:13-16 says "Now listen, you who say, "Today or tomorrow we will go to this or that city, spend a year there, carry on business and make money." Why, you do not even know what will happen tomorrow. What is your life? You are a mist that appears for a little while and then vanishes. Instead you ought to say, "If it is the Lord's will, we will live and do this or that." As it is, you boast in your arrogant schemes. All such boasting is evil." Probably the best posture to have regarding stewarding our time is to assume we don't have much left. How would your priorities and to-do lists change if you found out today that you had only one more year of life left to live? What would you put on your bucket list? Who would you want to reconcile or reconnect with? What steps would you take to put your estate in order for the sake of your loved ones? How would you approach God and further cultivate your relationship with Him?

- Our money and possessions. I Timothy 6:6-10 states that "godliness with contentment is great gain. For we brought nothing into the world, and we can take nothing out of it. But if we have food and clothing, we will be content with that. Those who want to get rich fall into temptation and a trap and into many foolish and harmful desires that plunge people into ruin and destruction. For the love of money is a root of all kinds of evil. Some people, eager for money, have wandered from the faith and pierced themselves with many griefs." In stewarding our money and possessions rather than owning, we escape the trap of entitlement and are able to find contentment no matter how much or how little we have. If God has entrusted you with much as a business manager or entrepreneur, be sure you treat people well and be generous with them, understanding that God has been generous with you. Be charitable and hospitable, sharing what you have with others, knowing that you will be judged by God according to the measure of your *relationships* rather than your possessions. So what charitable causes are dearest to your heart and to God's purposes for you? What would extravagant giving to this cause look like in your situation? What are you investing in now that will benefit future generations?

- Our decisions, plans, and hearts. Isaiah 55:8-9 says, "'For my thoughts are not your thoughts, neither are your ways my ways, declares the Lord.' For as the heavens are higher than the earth, so are my ways higher than your ways and my thoughts than your thoughts.'" As stewards rather than owners of our thoughts and plans, we are called firstly to be in constant communication with God through prayer. This extra step, particularly when faced with a major decision, is the most worthwhile investment you can make. In acknowledging His ownership over our futures, He will help us avoid major pitfalls and keep us steadily focused on our unique purpose. Only by taking the time to be focused and purpose-driven can we reduce the power of distractions and be wiser in our choices. As stewards we are also called to life-long learning and personal development. Done the right way and with a heart of gratitude, choosing to increase your knowledge will draw you closer to His heart and deepen your appreciation of His creation and your place in it.

This week reflect on the difference between ownership and stewardship. Where might you carry an entitlement mentality that needs to be surrendered? As you journal you plans, prayers, feelings and fears, commit them to God, your true and loving Landlord, and watch Him multiply your blessing and influence as you seek to steward diligently all He has entrusted to your care.

THE POWER OF WORDS

Have you ever been deeply touched by a great singer's performance? What makes their gift so powerful? Where does the talent end and the training begin? I've recently been studying the voice and have found many interesting points worth sharing. Did you know that professional singers are trained to breathe differently? They may have all the talent in the world, but if they don't learn to breathe from their lower abdominal cavity rather than their chest, they won't be able to support the greater breath necessary to take their gift to the next level. Singers are also very aware of how their mouth and throat serve to give their words optimal resonance and vibration. They know themselves well, understanding the unique sound they've been given to use. Through extended practice, the singer gradually becomes an expert on the dynamic interplay between vocal tone, word articulation, and emotional expression in order to communicate their message optimally. The end result is a beautiful dance of breath, word, and spirit that together have the power to nourish and engage a captive audience. In short, natural musical talent is not enough to communicate a message with beauty and power. It must also be developed through training and focus.

I'd like to propose that this principle is equally true with the spoken word. All of us have words, and all of us have an audience to communicate with. We too must learn to master the important dynamic between breath, word, and spirit as we engage in conversation with those around us so that it does good, and not evil. Colossians 4:6 says, "Let your conversation be always full of grace, seasoned with salt, so that you may know how to answer everyone." Like a singer, not only do our actual words carry meaning, but the way we package and present them communicates as well. As humans created in the image of God, our words have spiritual power to build up or break down, as we shall see.

Remember that in Genesis 1, God *spoke* the world into being. Think about that for a moment. A declaration creating tangible things. Amazing! Hebrews 11:3 says that by faith we understand that the universe was formed at God's *command*, so that what is seen was not made out of what was visible. Even in physics we know that the smallest particle is the photon, or *sound wave*. Makes sense, doesn't it? God spoke, and his very words emitted photons into the empty darkness that he then expertly fashioned together to form our world. Incredible!

And yet words, especially God's words, are much more than just sounds. Words need breath and spirit to be truly life-transforming. We find God's spirit of wisdom personified in Proverbs 8:22-31. "The Lord brought me forth as the first of his works, before his deeds of old; I was formed long ages ago, at the very beginning, when the world came to be. I was there when he set the heavens in place, when he marked out the horizon on the face of the deep." For God to speak creation into existence, His words had to be accompanied by divine design and counsel in order to accomplish their task.

Likewise, we as humans made in His image have power in our words to create or destroy. Proverbs 18:21 says "the tongue has the power of life and death, and those who love it will eat its fruit." James 3:2 warns that "we all stumble in many ways. Anyone who is never at fault in what they say is perfect, able to keep their whole body in check." In other words, this same crucial element of spiritual wisdom God used to create the world is also needed by us, or else our words are no more life-giving than a 'resounding gong or a clanging cymbal' (1 Cor. 13:1). Like a beautiful singer, wisdom in speech is that key design element behind the presentation and timing of words, word choice, and tone of voice. There is even wisdom in not speaking at all, but rather allowing a dramatic silence to do its work.

In order to cultivate human speech that builds up rather than destroys, I find it helpful to picture each member of the Trinity issuing a different part. I like to think that God the Father, our Creator, provides us with the physical breath in our lungs, as we find in Genesis 2:7. Without our life breath from Him, speech isn't possible. So when you're next tempted to say something hastily, instead take a deep breath, thanking God for it like a gift. Then decide if what you wanted to say is still worth saying. Next, I picture our Saviour Jesus, as the Word who became Flesh (John 1), giving us the words we speak. It was Jesus who used human speech to raise the dead, to pray to the Father, and to teach about the Kingdom, so we can, too. Finally, I see the Holy Spirit as the One who fills us with the wisdom we so desperately need to ensure our words act as life-giving water. Particularly when we need courage to speak the truth in love, the Holy Spirit can give us the wisdom to be both bold and compassionate, in the proper way at the proper time.

Feeling overwhelmed by the weight of this power you hold? Take heart - we find several Bible heroes quivering at the prospect of speaking. First there is Moses, whom God called to deliver the Israelites from slavery. "Moses said to the Lord, 'Pardon your servant, Lord. I have never been eloquent, neither in the past nor since you have spoken to your servant. I am slow of speech and tongue.' The Lord said to him, 'Who gave human beings their mouths? Who makes them deaf or mute? Who gives them sight or makes them blind? Is it not I, the Lord? Now go; I will help you speak and will teach you what to say'" (Exodus 4:10-12).

The great prophet Isaiah, upon receiving a heavenly vision of angels surrounding the Lord on his throne, cried out, "'Woe to me! I am ruined! For I am a man of unclean lips, and I live among a people of unclean lips, and my eyes have seen the King, the Lord Almighty.' Then one of the seraphim flew to me with a live coal in his hand, which he had taken with tongs from the altar. With it he touched my mouth and said, 'See, this has touched your lips, your guilt is taken away and your sin atoned for.'" (Isaiah 6:5-7)

The prophet Jeremiah as well, when just a young man, shuddered at the prospect of speaking for God. "'Alas, Sovereign Lord,' I said, 'I do not know how to speak; I am too young.' But the Lord said to me, 'Do not say, 'I am too young.' You must go to everyone I send you to and say whatever I command you. Do not be afraid of them, for I am with you and will rescue you,' declares the Lord. Then the Lord reached out his hand and touched my mouth and said to me, 'I have put my words in your mouth." (Jeremiah 1:6-9)

Yes, it is good to remember the weight of the power that our words carry, but also remember we aren't meant to carry it alone. In each of these instances, God offered reassurance to his servants, and he will do the same for you. Whether you need words to worship, to encourage someone, or to speak truth over yourself, remember our quivering heroes and God's response to them. Also remember that He is the Divine

Singer who rejoices over you (Zeph. 3:17b), so picture Him showering you with a thundering resonance of lyrical melody from deep within His being. Even now as He fills your lungs with air, keep yourself open and willing to allow His breath, words, and spirit to overflow from your mouth.

This week, bring God all your words and lay them at his feet. He longs to forgive you, cleanse your lips, and put His words in your mouth. Ask the Holy Spirit for a greater measure of wisdom to discern how to package your words, so that they are always life-giving to the hearer. Then journal words of thanksgiving and worship back to God, committing to keep His praise ever on your lips.

Plans and Prayers

In your journal, take the time to write down your plans and goals for the coming month of May.

What do you love the most about spring? Take time to celebrate the newness of life all around you and the God of new beginnings, and record what you feel him saying to you.

What are some practical ways you could more fully embrace the creativity God has given you?

What concerns are on your heart today that you need to speak His promises over, as He gives you the breath, words and wisdom to do so?

What things do you need to confess to Him, and thank Him for?

Feelings and Fears

What are you feeling today? Joyful? Burdened? Frustrated? Numb?

In navigating your current battle, do you feel more like a prisoner of war or a war hero right now?

Write out how you feel before God – He's been in your shoes and knows what you're going through.

What if, by pushing through fear, you found Jesus on the other side?

Freely journal about whatever comes to mind, as an act of surrendering it all to Him.

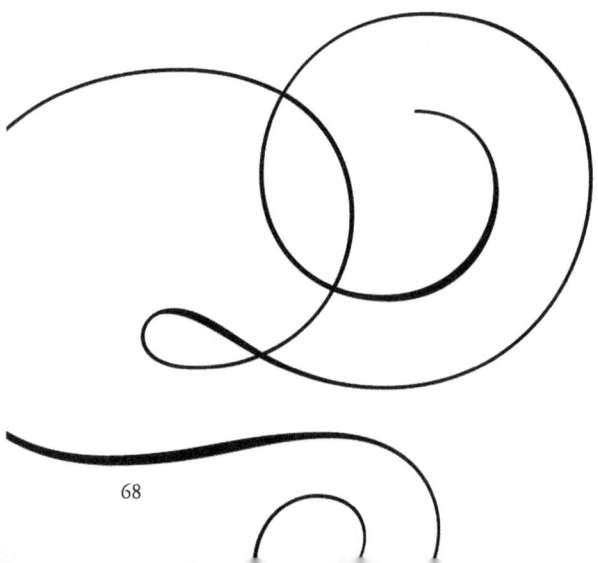

May

THE MARY-MARTHA BALANCE

There is a familiar story in the Bible about two sisters: Mary and Martha. They were friends of Jesus, and He would often visit their home whenever he passed through their village. If you have a sister, you know how very different sisters can be. These two sisters were no exception:

> As Jesus and his disciples were on their way, he came to a village where a woman named Martha opened her home to him. She had a sister called Mary, who sat at the Lord's feet listening to what he said. But Martha was distracted by all the preparations that had to be made. She came to him and asked, "Lord, don't you care that my sister has left me to do the work by myself? Tell her to help me!" The Lord answered, "Martha, Martha, you are worried and upset about many things, but few things are needed – or indeed only one. Mary has chosen what is better, and it will not be taken away from her. (Luke 10:38-42)

Are you a Mary or a Martha? This well-known story often paints Martha in a dismal light, and yet she deeply loved her Lord. It clearly states that she opened her home to him. What got her off track was allowing herself to become *distracted* from her purpose, causing her to cross the line from serving the Lord's need to serving her own pride. We've all been guilty of this, even in church ministry settings. There is so much kingdom work to do, yet it matters a great deal to God what we choose to do and in what manner we choose to do it. The only way to discern how the Lord wants us to serve Him is to be like Mary: to spend time sitting at His feet, enjoying His presence, and listening to His words. Unlike Martha, Mary's eyes were focused on Jesus and not on herself. In other words, the I's have it: the *Intimacy* and *Identity* we glean from His *Image* is the only way to achieve true *Insight*. Only insight from the Father can help you resist the world's daily grind with its standards of success, which can so easily overwhelm you with worry as it did Martha. Purposeful activity is healthy, but we need to find a Mary-Martha balance.

It all starts with Intimacy. Jesus said, "Many will say to me on that day, 'Lord, Lord, did we not prophesy in your name and in your name drive out demons and in your name perform many miracles?' Then I will tell them plainly, 'I never *knew* you. Away from me, you evildoers!'" (Matt. 7:22-23). The Greek word used here for 'knew' means an intimate knowing, as a husband knows his wife. Truly, many well-intentioned Christians have done incredible things in His name, yet they were done in their own strength and according to their own agenda. They never took the time to truly know the Person behind the power in His name, and so failed to serve the Lord through their lack of intimacy. They are essentially Marthas.

Intimacy leads us to identity. Only when we define ourselves by Who we belong to and what He has created us to be will we find a purpose to pursue that is truly life-giving and of service to our Lord. We were never meant to scatter our efforts randomly, hoping to do some good to someone somewhere. Rather we were meant to stop and take aim, focus our eyes on Him, and then put our identity into motion. I'm sure Mary wasn't an idle or lazy sister, or else Martha wouldn't have been so surprised at having to serve Jesus by herself. Yet Mary knew that His very presence was a gift and felt the best use of her time at that moment was to be a quiet, captive audience. Likewise, we should work diligently, but always have a listening ear towards the Master for direction and insight. Having Martha's hands and Mary's heart: that's the Mary-Martha balance.

This week, meditate on the story of Mary and Martha, and times when you have acted as one or the other. As you journal your plans, prayers, feelings, and fears, ask God to reveal greater insight into the purpose He designed you to fill, and the person He designed you to become.

Mothers & Mentors

Spring is my favourite time of year – particularly the month of May. It symbolizes new birth, new possibilities, and new hope. It's no wonder, therefore, that we also celebrate mothers during this month. Being a mother carries with it tremendous creative potential, and from God's perspective, it is not limited to only birthing and raising your own children. We all know what it means to be a daughter, and how our mothers had a profound impact on the women we grew to become. But many have also benefited from other women who have chosen to encourage and speak into their lives. I had the wonderful opportunity recently of serving as a mentor in my church's Woman To Woman mentoring program. It was a beautiful experience that really stretched and challenged me, and definitely made me stronger. As a Christian woman pursues spiritual maturity, God will open doors of opportunity for her to become a 'mother' to the next spiritual generation, whether through a formal program at a church or a burden for someone that the Lord has placed on her heart. From serving the Lord for many years, she will know very well how many 'pearls' the Lord has allowed her past trials to create in her, and with authority and determination she can speak through her brokenness into the life of another. It is an intentional choice that requires time and energy as well as vision and insight. Ask any such mother, though, and they'll tell you it's so much more than just teaching. The Bible says in 1 Corinthians 4:15, "Even if you had ten thousand [teachers] in Christ, you do not have many [mothers], for in Christ Jesus I became your [mother] through the gospel." This was written by the apostle Paul, who knew great suffering in his life. Yet his passion to see others come to Jesus and to reach spiritual maturity was fueled by the heart of a loving parent, not just the mind of a teacher.

Teachers simply pass on what they know; mothers pass on who they are.

So for those of you who have not seen the fulfillment of your heart's desire to birth and raise natural children, or you are feeling the ache of an empty nest, I would offer you Isaiah 54:1: "'Sing, barren woman, you who never bore a child; burst into song, shout for joy, you who were never in labour; because more are the children of the desolate woman than of her who has a husband,' says the Lord." God views spiritual mothering as even more important than physical mothering. So whether you have natural children or not, the experience of being a spiritual mother to someone in need of guidance will always be worth the effort. You may feel strong reluctance and opposition at times, but through your maturity you will recognize any tiredness, frustration, or inconvenience for what it is and use it to further refine your character.

Being a mother takes all you have to give.

So take heart - the fulfillment, joy and sense of purpose that comes from creating in, and giving to, those around you will confirm the importance of the role that you play. Happy Mother's Day!

This week, journal about the mothers you have known in your life, both physical and spiritual. What qualities and characteristics did they pass on to you? Also record the ways in which a mother has hurt or hindered you, as a means of releasing it to God and asking Him to help you forgive her. How might you seek out a younger woman in need of spiritual mothering, to offer encouragement, comfort, and guidance? Record some ideas and names that come to mind, and your plans and prayers for them.

FOR SUCH A TIME AS THIS:
THE ESTHER EFFECT

There is a book in the Bible about a queen named Esther. Esther was a Jew, but she wasn't queen of the Jews. She was born a poor, orphaned girl living in the hostile foreign land of Persia. She was raised by her older cousin Mordecai, who honoured the Lord and instilled in Esther a reverence for God and a love for her people. Her Hebrew name was 'Hadassah', which means 'myrtle'. The myrtle plant has delicate, shiny, dark green leaves that release fragrance, particularly when crushed. Like Esther, the myrtle plant represented peace and thanksgiving to the Jewish people (Zechariah 1:11) and would come to symbolize

Esther's beautiful fragrance being released over her husband and her exiled people as their Queen.

It's interesting to note that God is never mentioned in the book of Esther. This doesn't mean that God was absent, but that the author of the book perhaps wished to spotlight and contrast the different characters' changes in fortune so that the hand of the Lord could be indirectly proclaimed. The particular favour Esther experienced and the perfect timing of events could not have happened by chance. Maybe you know someone who defines their circumstances by chance, fate, and luck, and you are unsure of how to direct them to seeing the Lord's hand. The book of Esther addresses this mindset on a level that keeps the reader's attention, but also makes them want to dig deeper into the mysterious Esther effect.

The Bible says that Esther was beautiful, pleasing even the king's attendants and winning their favour. Yet before approaching the king for his approval, Esther had to complete twelve months of beauty treatments. Preparation is important. Whether it is an external beauty regimen or an internal molding of the heart, we must be prepared to prepare. When Esther did finally approach the king, he was "attracted to Esther more than to any of the other women, and she won his favour and approval more than the rest" (Esther 2:17). This result was the Lord's work. Our job is to diligently prepare, His job is to dramatically provide.

Once declared Queen, Esther job was not done. A plot had been devised to kill all the Jews in the land, and Mordecai persuaded Esther to do all she could to save them in his famous question, "who knows but that you have come to your royal position for such a time as this?" (Esther 4:14). Once again, Esther needed to prepare herself for an audience with the king, for she knew if she approached him uninvited, she would be put to death. Have you ever felt God calling you to do something risky? Esther certainly did, and she knew she needed to prepare, and trust for God's provision. She had all her friends and attendants fast and pray with her for three days. She then carefully dressed in her finest robes to approach the king. Again, her diligent preparation brought the Lord's dramatic provision, and the king extended Esther a warm welcome. Though still hungry and distressed, Esther felt she needed to demonstrate her respect, honour, and inner beauty to her king before making her request on behalf of her people. She invited the king to two lavish banquets, which served to nourish her marriage as well as herself. Only then did she plead with the king, falling at his feet weeping, to put an end to the evil plan in place to kill the Jews. The king extended his gold scepter to Esther and she arose and stood before him triumphant.

What a beautiful story! An exiled orphan girl with a divine purpose upon her life rose to be queen over a pagan land and wife to a foolish, conceited man. Yet she maintained her integrity, humility, and true identity, demonstrated great wisdom and restraint, and respectfully served those around her. A truly inspiring example of feminine courage and beauty, inside and out. That's the Esther effect.

This week, read the story of Esther in the Bible, imagining yourself in her position. How might you follow her example of integrity and restraint within the pagan culture that surrounds you today? How might you honour a dishonourable person in your life, simply because they are made in the image of God? As ideas and names come to mind, add them to your list of plans, prayers, feelings, and fears, asking God to help you to see this needy world through His eyes.

THE PROVERBIAL WOMAN:
REFLECTIONS ON PROVERBS 31

As long as I can remember, I've longed for greater understanding about what it means to be a woman of God. As a little girl, I would admire the women in my church who seemed to personify what I was looking for – those who sang beautifully, dressed elegantly, or entertained graciously. Today, I'm still inspired by these attributes in the women around me but have come to understand that they don't *define* what a woman of God is, but rather *reveal* the particular kind of woman that I aspire to be.

And then there is Proverbs 31. Without a doubt, this passage of Scripture has influenced my understanding of womanhood, but to a lesser degree than most. With living examples readily available for me to study, Proverbs 31 only ever stood as a shadowy backdrop. However, many women I know have really wrestled with shame and frustration, for good reason, after studying this passage. There are the feminists, who view this chapter as degrading and restricting. Then there are those who, through coming to faith later in life, didn't have any role models of strong godly women to learn from during their formative years. They were simply directed to read this passage and apply it to their lives the best they could, as a woman's standard for Godly living.

So in light of the misinterpretations this passage has known and to serve as a healing balm for those who experience angst and despair by my simply mentioning Proverbs 31, let me offer some contextual aids.

The first thing we need to remember is the meaning of the word 'proverb'. Something that is 'proverbial' is an unattainable standard – created by design to serve as an archetype. Therefore, the Proverbs 31 woman is *not a real person*. Comparing yourself to her is like comparing yourself to those airbrushed models who appear on magazine covers! The image you see is not what that person really looks like, but an altered representation designed to communicate a particular agenda. So it is with the Proverbs 31 woman. Each verse is carefully constructed to communicate a message to a certain audience. So, what is the message, and who is the audience? Keep reading!

At the beginning of the chapter we learn that this text was written by a mother to her son – a son who is a king. Though we don't know his age, we can guess that he was a teenager or slightly younger. Essentially a young man who bore the weight of great responsibility and great promise for the future. Much hung in the balance at this moment, and his mother's heart was divinely inspired to train her royal son to choose a wife wisely. Temptations abounded - drunkenness, apathy, lust – and she knew that only with wisdom could a king be truly noble. How much more, then, was this mother concerned about the character of her future daughter-in-law? For not only would she be a queen, but also the primary influence in her son's life. His ability to make this crucial decision well was paramount. Now, in this light, how could today's women read Proverbs 31:10-31 differently? What kind of woman would you advise your royal son to marry?

Very good, you say. The target audience is not women at all, but young men in need of guidance on what it looks like to choose wisely. And even feminists must agree that he is charged with choosing an equal – a true partner in life whom he can praise – and not a slave or an object for his own pleasure.

So, if that is the intended audience, what is the underlying message? Well, if you examine the passage in the original Hebrew, it takes the form of an acrostic poem called a chiasm. A chiasm has a central focus that all other verses point to, which in this instance is verse 23: "Her husband is respected at the city gate, where he takes his seat among the elders of the land". How interesting! So not only is this passage *not* meant to be read by women as a measuring stick for themselves, but the young Hebrew men who originally read it would have understood clearly that the point of finding such a woman was so that they *themselves* would be honoured and respected by all! (This wasn't a guarantee, of course, since it's just a proverb, but it's a good case in point for us women to recognize how much men crave respect, if so presented as their reward for acting wisely.) The secondary message is hidden earlier in the book of Proverbs. Chapters 8 & 9 contain the metaphor of Lady Wisdom, which the reader (again, a young man) is implored to cling to. This final passage of Proverbs, then, serves to echo and reinforce this theme. Consider Prov. 8:11, which reads "for wisdom is more precious than rubies, and nothing you desire can compare with her" as well as Prov. 9:1-2: "Wisdom has built her house; she has set up its seven pillars. She has prepared her meat and mixed her wine; she has also set her table." How alike are these themes to the Proverbs 31 woman, who "is worth far more than rubies" (v. 10) and "who watches over the affairs of her household" (v. 27)? Surely the echo was noticed by the original audience and can still be by us today.

So, what about you and me, then, as twenty-first-century women? Are we then given permission to dismiss that check in our spirit whenever we read this passage? I would say no. With its principles of wisdom and noble character themes, I believe there are things here for us to ponder even today. Verse 30 is key: "Charm is deceptive, and *beauty is fleeting*; but a woman who fears the Lord is to be praised." This theme is picked up in the New Testament in I Peter 3:3-4: "Your beauty should not come from outward adornment, rather it should be that of your inner self, the *unfading beauty* of a gentle and quiet spirit, which is of great worth in God's sight." We each have enduring beauty on the inside in need of cultivation. Ask the Lord what that check in your spirit means and what He wants you to do about it. Set shame and frustration aside and begin with one step. When read between the lines, Proverbs 31 unearths many themes that today's Christian woman can ponder.

- Bringing her husband good, honour, and respect
- Working eagerly and not grudgingly
- Being a source of wisdom and nourishment for her household
- Extending charity to those in need
- Fearing the Lord rather than the future
- Having perseverance and keeping the big picture in view
- Growing in creativity, compassion, and strength throughout her life

In reading Proverbs 31, we also must recognize that our proverbial woman accomplished these things in different seasons of her life, *not all in the same year*. I like to think that when newly-married, she began selecting wool and flax, and spun on her spindle the items her and her coming children would need. When her children were small, her priority was getting up while it was night, feeding them and speaking wisdom into their lives. When her children were teenagers, she made garments and bed coverings, and began to sell some of her items to merchants. Once an empty-nester, she then had the time and means to purchase a field, plant a vineyard, and give generously to the poor. Neither lazy nor over-extended, neither busy nor bored, she didn't compare herself to other women nor feel she had to prove something. Her secret? *She knew her worth and identity in the eyes of the Lord.* It was only His opinion that truly mattered, only His strengthening words that truly fulfilled. Only with the Lord as her focus could she persevere through the ups and downs in order to live a life of true nobility. And that's what the book of Proverbs is all about: training a person to 'reign in life' no matter their social status or level of education. It's training its readers how to have a regal mindset and a noble heart.

So, look around you – Proverbs 31 women can be found everywhere, if you take the time to look. Ask the Lord to show you what women you might seek to learn from, and what particular qualities he wants you to work on in this season. We all fall short of proverbial perfection, so there's a good chance that you'll learn more from her weaknesses than her strengths! But embrace her flawed example as you embrace your own, recognizing that you're both Proverbs 31 women in-the-making and worthy of winning a king's heart.

This week, read Proverbs 31 again in light of its true context, and pray that the young men you know would desire to marry a woman of such noble character. Then, journal your honest feelings about this passage, both positive and negative, offering them to God. He knows your struggles and frustrations, but longs to form in you a royal heart after His own. Allow Him as your King and Soulmate to captivate your imagination once again, and receive the affirmation and praise deserving of your royal status as His bride.

THE AUTOGRAPH

The place was packed. The lights had dimmed. The anticipation was palpable. Any moment now the music would begin and the one we all had come to see would arrive on stage.

Isn't it exciting to have your favourite singer give a concert in your area? In my case, it was seeing Michael W. Smith in concert several years ago. He's been writing songs for so long now, that his first record was actually a *record*. And since I happened to own one such vinyl record of his, I decided to bring it along with me to the concert. I knew he didn't sign autographs, but I thought it would be fun to show the album to my friends. Of course, once I began to show it around, everyone started suggesting I try to get it signed! So before the concert began, I went to the foyer with album in hand, and ran into another friend of mine who was working backstage. She was a big fan herself, and so she took the album, promising to see what she could do. All that remained was to return to my seat and wait. I'll admit, I didn't pay much attention to the opening act. At long last, intermission was called, and my friend reappeared - with a *signed* album in hand! She told me that he was so floored about someone still owning an original vinyl album that he just had to sign it! I was in speechless amazement, which brought my anticipation of the actual concert to a whole new level. It turned out to be one of the most thrilling evenings of my life.

And it was all made possible by an old, used record album that I happened to notice at the bottom of a dusty pile at my local thrift store last year. I had recently began a small record collection just for the nostalgia, and so took a brief moment that day to browse through the eclectic music history that had been donated. Never had the phrase, 'someone's trash is another's treasure', been so real to me as I unearthed that gem from the back of the pile and freed it from its dust bunny enslavement. I quickly paid the pocket-change ransom required and took it home to join my other treasures.

All the records in my small collection have a similar redemption story; and I love listening to them and reflecting on how I've returned to them their usefulness and dignity. But no other record in my collection so far has been bestowed as great an honour as the one that was personally autographed. It's not like it was deserving of such an honour either, since it was clearly tattered and used, but Michael signed it simply because it was *his*. Do you ever feel tattered and used, and undeserving of God's love? The question shouldn't be about who you are, but *whose* you are. We all have the same Creator, but not everyone has allowed Him to autograph their life with the meaning, purpose, and value that only He can give.

And so in turn, we as Christians have a mandate that is two-fold. Firstly, to participate in social justice causes that help rescue people who feel discarded and worthless and give them back their usefulness and dignity. We all deserve to have a sense of belonging in our lives, and to know there are people who care. But government-run programs can do that, too. So we also have a second mission of pointing people to Jesus. All humans, including those of us in society who may have 'nice' lives – a nice job, a nice house, a nice family – are also in need of a help that is less evident. Just like a clean, neat record collection that is well cared-for and used, we may have function and dignity, but still lack *ownership*. Jesus paid the ransom required to buy us back, and believe me, it was a lot more than pocket-change. He gave up His life and died for you. Won't you allow Him to sign His name on the cover of your life? Trust me, recognizing your ownership will bring you more meaning, purpose and value than you ever thought possible.

So where is my signed album now? It's behind a glass frame, hanging on my wall. From such humble beginnings to such honour. It can be the same for you.

Take time to reflect and journal on what it means to have Jesus' 'autograph' on your life. Is it a large, pronounced script, visible to all? How might it remind you of your worth when you feel tattered and used?

> *When I first finished writing this article, I was prompted to submit it to Michael W. Smith's press agent for him to read. To my surprise and delight, I soon received confirmation that Michael himself read it and enjoyed it!*

Plans and Prayers

In your journal, take the time to write down your plans and goals for the coming month of June.

How have your reflections on motherhood and the female identity shaped how you see yourself as a woman? How have they shaped how you approach the roles you fill?

What concerns are on your heart today that you need to write out as prayer requests to God? Looking back in your journal, what answers to prayer can you thank Him for?

What women in your life inspire you the most? Who do you inspire? How might you be more intentional in allowing a mentor (or mentee) into the daily rhythm of your life?

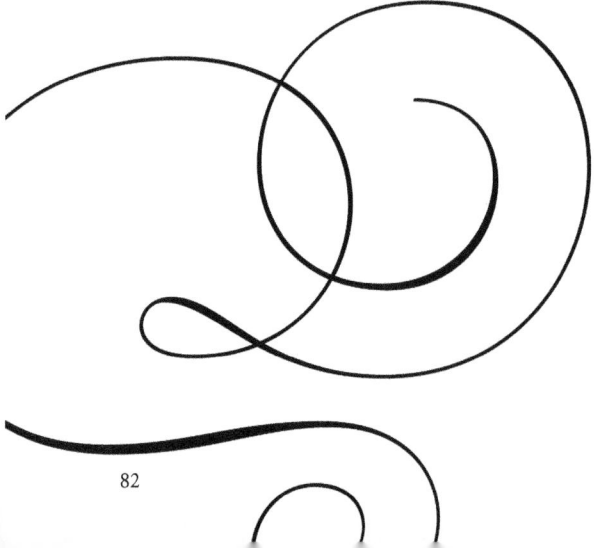

Feelings and Fears

What are you feeling today? Joyful? Burdened? Frustrated? Numb?

What's most overwhelming to you about being a Christian woman?

Write out how you feel before God. Let Him shower you with His grace and love.

How did your mother's failures and struggles define you?

Freely journal about whatever comes to mind, as an act of surrendering it all to Him.

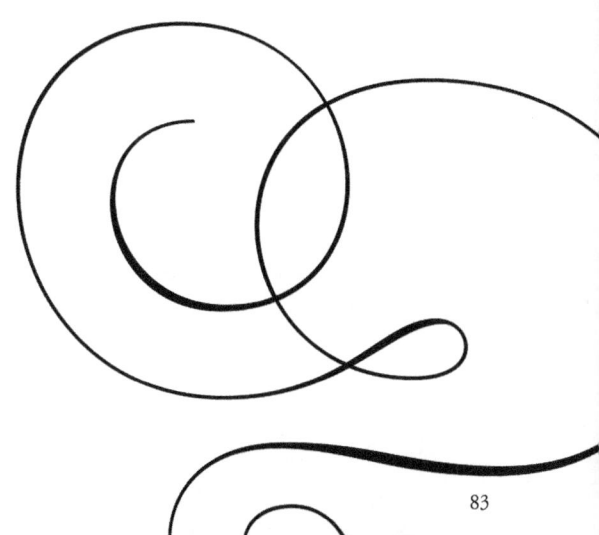

June

Roses:
Soft Blooms, Sharp Thorns

It's been said that the most beautiful flower is the rose. Yet roses bloom only in certain seasons, and they require specific nutrients and conditions in order to fully flower as they are meant to do. They also produce thorns meant to protect and guard the growing offshoot from damage. To me, this raises the question: "Is it really worth all that effort?" Of course it is. You see, rose blooms are not just appendages of beauty; they are instruments of reproduction. The bush not only cares about survival and growth in the here and now, but it also cares about cultivating the next generation.

Our society today wants us to live in the here-and-now moment all the time; to only consider ourselves or dream our own individual dreams for our lifetime. Yet as a wise person once said, your dream is too small if it only has to do with you. Cultivating your dream – your rose – isn't selfish, so long as it is meant to enable and equip future generations to rise up once you are gone. So dream big! Use the extensive resources at your disposal, channel them into the specific dream, ministry, or promise the Lord has given you, and go for it with all your might for the sake of the kingdom now and into the future.

There are so many different types of roses. They vary in colour, size, fragrance, and blooming season. There are those that climb, and those that stay low to the ground. Those that are particularly prone to infection, those that prefer dry, wet, sandy or acidic soil, those that can tolerate harsh wind and cold and those that need a great deal of warmth and sunlight to bloom. Like rose bushes, we also have different needs, strengths, and qualities that are each beautiful in unique and complementary ways. It takes risk and energy to bloom; to showcase publicly what God has given us and reveal the soft beauty we possess. It takes courage and vulnerability, making us susceptible to comparison based on what our roses look like and the effort it took for us to make them. When our confidence wavers, we are too quick to seek praise and affirmation from those around us instead of from the One who is our true source of life. Remember, whatever your dream is, the ultimate goal is to live a life consumed with praising the One who gave you your rose and stewarding its use and beauty wisely.

And then, there are the thorns. Thorns on rose stems serve as protection from predators, both of which are the result of the Fall (Genesis 3:18). If we as women were each a rose, how would we respond and behave differently if we no longer felt we needed protection or needed to conceal ourselves against anything? Before the Fall – before thorns existed – was when women and roses were created. They were originally created by God to respond and behave with childlike innocence and heartfelt abandon to the glory and honour of their Creator. With nothing painful or sinister known to them, they displayed and celebrated beauty and tenderness with a vulnerability that would be shocking today. Yet now, we are at war. We have suffered wounds and inflicted them on others. The rosebushes of many hearts are gnarled, stunted, and malnourished, exhibiting ugly and painful thorns grown to try and protect the delicate life inside. A rose may still bloom, but harsh exposures and infestations bring it prematurely to the ground. The struggle is so constant and so real that many hearts resign themselves and their dreams to failure and give up thinking of the future or of hoping for more. Proverbs 24:30-31 says, "I went past the field of the sluggard; past the vineyard of someone who lacked a heart of wisdom. Thorns had come up everywhere, the ground was covered with weeds, and the stone wall was in ruins." Life is tough, and it feels futile to try and keep going. Our hearts become beaten down with busyness, worry and regret, and we often stop dreaming just to save energy.

And yet that is exactly why Jesus came – to bring us true life and life more abundantly (John 10:10). The Apostle Paul endured an abiding 'thorn in the flesh' (2 Corinthians 12:7) and yet wrote most of the New Testament by remaining committed to the grand vision Jesus had called him to. When you confess Jesus as your Lord and Saviour, you also give your heart permission to dream big despite the struggle and obstacles in your way. You give it permission to long and prepare for the day when all the earth is exposed and we are made fully alive, without risk of pain, rejection, shame or misunderstanding. The coming Kingdom of God is one of complete redemption: mankind, animals, plants, and the very land itself. The crown of thorns Jesus wore at his crucifixion symbolized the extent of the curse that He died to eliminate. Isaiah 55:13 prophesies, "Instead of the thorn will come up the cypress; instead of the brier shall come up the myrtle; and it shall make a name for the Lord, an everlasting sign that shall not be cut off." Ezekiel 28:24 echoes, "No longer will the people of Israel have malicious neighbours who are painful briers and sharp thorns. Then they will know that I am the Sovereign Lord." On that day, we shall be clothed in His righteousness, and our hearts will flower with radiance and worshipful abandon once again. So embrace your dream today, and His promise of a true and thornless rose in bloom tomorrow.

This week, reflect and journal about what harsh circumstances are preventing your rose from blooming fully. What thorns are pressing against your flesh that He is actually using to protect you and promote your rose to bloom? As the Master Gardener, ask Him to show you the bigger purpose for your rose, as we approach the coming of summer.

Beauty has no Worry Warts

Why do we worry? Where does it come from? Jesus said, "Do not worry about your life, what you will eat or drink; or about your body, what you will wear. Is not life more than food, and the body more than clothes? Look at the birds of the air; they do not sow or reap or store away in barns, and yet your heavenly Father feeds them. Are you not much more valuable than they?" (Matt. 6:25-26)

The word 'worry' in the original Greek means 'to be pulled apart'. By worrying, we try to bridge the great divide between what we can control in life and what we cannot. Jesus has given us each a kingdom purpose from His Father, and he commands us to "seek first His kingdom and His righteousness, and all these things will be given to you as well" (Matt. 6:33). It all sounds so simple: work diligently at what you can control and leave what you can't control to Him. So is it the simplicity of it that makes us stumble? Have we become too busy, too proud, or too intellectual to ponder how tiny birds demonstrate God's care for us?

By believing in God as our Creator we also must believe in God as our Sustainer, for why would God neglect that which He has created? With every heartbeat and with every breath, we are experiencing the sustaining hand of God. As little girls, we marveled at simply waking up each morning and celebrating the smallest miracles of nature. Now that we are women, what happened to our trusting hearts and eyes full of wonder? I'm sure you used to play being a grown-up when you were little; so why not play being a child now? Jesus is encouraging us to reclaim our childlike faith and stand in awe once again at His sustaining hand directing our lives.

So what are we supposed to learn from these birds? In the first place, birds are busy creatures. They gather food, build their nests, and care for their young. They have a desire to survive just as much as you do. Yet the difference is that they regard all they receive as a gift from His hand and feel no sense of entitlement to anything. Why do we allow our pride to dictate to us all we feel we deserve? The next time you see a bird, think about this: you deserve only death, and only through God's gracious mercy have you been given abundant life.

So where does worry come from? It comes from humanity's selfish desire for full control apart from God. We want to make our own priorities, achieve our own dreams, and live forever healthy and strong. We seldom want to face our limitations or weaknesses. Worry is therefore the struggle we bring upon ourselves when we sense that the success of our plans is really out of our hands. We sense we were meant for more, and long for life's immediate fulfillment, yet we worry whenever we try to attain this greatness on our own.

Worry is not only unnecessary, it is damaging. Worry causes warts to grow in the beautifully pure complexion God has designed for you. Warts are contagious growths formed on a broken area of skin. The weaknesses and limitations in your life were meant to bring God greater glory yet worry has brought forth ugly bumps there instead. By worrying, you are essentially telling God you would rather have warts for their protection instead of the tender beauty of a pure complexion; that you want to achieve your own ideas in your own time rather than waiting on His. Are you ready to give back full control to God? All those little things that keep you up at night, are you ready to surrender them fully to God's plan, and let Him give you back your beauty sleep? Worry habits are hard to break, so it will take a continuous, conscious effort to resist picking that burden back up from where you laid it at His feet. Yet the beauty that God has designed for you is more radiant than you can imagine, for "not even Solomon in all his splendor was dressed like one of these" (Matthew 6:29).

This week, read Matthew 6:25-26 slowly several times, allowing its deep truth to penetrate your heart. Ask God to reveal to you the root behind your greatest fears and write down all that comes to mind. What trials and disappointments have allowed distrust to grow worry warts in your life? What would it look like to fully trust God to provide for your every need? Journal freely, reconnecting your heart to the childlike innocence you once knew.

Daddy's Girl

Were you a daddy's girl growing up? Did you have a special relationship with your father? Were there times when he would let you get away with things that mom never would? This was certainly true of my childhood. I never doubted my dad's love and care for me, and I always felt valued and provided for. But perhaps you had a different experience – one that was neglectful or even scary. As little girls, our feelings of worth and value, as well as our spiritual well-being, came from our fathers. Our concept of our Heavenly Father was directly related to how healthy our relationship was to our earthly father. If your relationship with your earthly father was strained or non-existent, your concept of a father may be quite negative or painful. Because your father lacked the qualities of a king, you never felt like a princess. This doesn't mean you aren't one, though. God sent His Son Jesus to pay the price required to adopt you into His family. Your real Father is a mighty King of love and compassion, who made you and who calls you His beautiful daughter. You've been a princess all along, but this identity has been locked inside your heart all this time. Only by allowing God to unlock your heart can your true self as a Daddy's girl be fully revealed.

Yes, I had a wonderful childhood, but even as a daddy's girl, I was still unprepared for my venture into the outside world. First, there was public school. I became very fearful once I began to experience the big, scary world outside and the hostile people in it. I knew I was safe and loved at home, but I was getting a different message when I ventured outside its walls. I felt tremendous pressure to do and strive – instead of just be. And I felt alone. I believed in God, but I was too young to truly understand that He was with me everywhere I went and that He wanted to fight my battles for me. I didn't know I had value simply because I existed, or that I could trust Him with my heart.

Most of you I'm sure can relate to feeling lonely as a child; the big, scary world that you were afraid was going to swallow you up if you didn't learn to tough it out. Perhaps you even felt this to a greater degree because your home life was in turmoil as well. You had no safe haven at all. All your vulnerability was exchanged for a suit of armor. You learned to perform to please. Acquiring that mindset at a young age caused you emotional strain that perhaps you bottled up for years. Begin to let God in to the pain of your past right now. The wounds or neglect you suffered were not your fault. You were not meant to strive to gain affection. Please believe that God saw you and loved you then just because you were you, and He offers you healing and a journey of restoration and freedom starting today – if you will open your heart to Him. Please take some time to reflect on your own childhood, and then give it over to God.

As I grew, I continued learning about God and His love, but I still found God an abstract concept that was hard to reconcile with my daily life and school work. In high school, I felt drawn to scientific studies and excelled at courses that required concrete, logical thinking. The pressure to strive and perform continued to build. God was always there, but I pictured Him solely as a tender Father of love and compassion, like my dad, and not as a mighty warrior willing and capable of taking my fears and hurts upon himself. I was still battling the world alone, and I felt I had to forfeit something just to survive – my heart.

As I'm sure you remember, it's extremely difficult being a preteen girl. I've always said that the most difficult phase of life for anyone – man or woman – is a girl going through puberty. At any other time of life (marriage, childbirth, a midlife crisis or terminal illness), there are support groups, friends, counselors, and many other resources available to help. But not when you're a twelve-year-old girl having to go to school every day fearing the looks, the whispering, and the very real chance that your period could start during gym class. It was your body and your emotions, but they were out of your control, and a hostile world was looking on waiting to devour you. I remember those feelings well: needing to hide myself and my heart just to survive. But it was more than just physical changes; I endured painful relational wounds as well. I watched girls around me compromise all they were raised to believe in just to gain a 'friend', only to have it end in back-stabbing and rumours being spread. I felt there was no one my age I could trust, and the concept of friendship took on a worthless, shallow connotation. Because of this, I endured an enclosed, survival-mode existence during high school. I would pray, but I never could really believe that God cared about my daily struggles, let alone desired to battle on my behalf. I valued the love of my parents and the respect of my teachers but functioned essentially like a robotic machine. I didn't want to think of myself as human, let alone a woman. I got good grades and won awards, but I was driven by fear, not by my heart – not the heart of God. I isolated myself more and more from the students around me to protect myself from bad influences and vice, but this kept the good influences away, too.

Looking back, I can see situations where God was gently urging me to open my heart again to friendship but it still took me many years to break free from my robotic, survival mode and allow my heart to trust again. Vulnerability and trust are keys to becoming a woman of God. The heart that you felt you had to forfeit in order to keep afloat in this evil world is what I hope you will try to reclaim as I have tried to do. That's what being a Daddy's girl really means.

Perhaps reading this, you think that my story is like a walk in the park compared to yours. You've done and experienced things that have severely dwarfed the way you view yourself and how you believe God must view you. Yet no one is ever too far away from the potential of becoming a Daddy's girl; it all starts with choosing to trust Him.

After I finished university, I moved away on my own to start my career. I made new friends on my own, went to church on my own, and bought a house on my own. I liked being independent, but I was also very lonely. The Lord was literally all I had. It was during these years on my own that the deep seeds of identity, purpose, creativity, and beauty that He had planted for me before I was born began to grow in my heart's garden, and I began to nourish them with spiritual intimacy and water them with my tears. New dreams, and ones I had long forgotten, began to spring up as I slowly began to learn and reclaim all I was created to be as a Daddy's girl. It was uncomfortable at times, as I was unsure how this deeply sensitive, vulnerable heart of mine would ever survive the daily daggers of everyday life. But God remained faithful, and His loving hand guided me through that lonely desert to a place where I was ready to step up and claim the dreams and potential that were there from the beginning, including writing this devotional book. It's a very special thing to be a Daddy's girl, and you can be one, too. It takes all you have, including all you are unwilling to forfeit, but it will totally transform your life. Welcome to the family!

This week, take time to journal about your dad, and about what a Father looks like in your life. You may even feel prompted to write a pretend letter to your dad, releasing all the emotions and dreams you always wanted to share with him but didn't. Whether you've suffered neglect or abuse, we've all experienced some pain from this relationship that needs to be acknowledged and redeemed by our Heavenly Father. Ask Him to reveal to you His heart, and the tremendous love and pride He feels for you, his own precious daughter. Journal your plans, prayers, feelings, and fears to him this week as if you were a little girl again, sitting on daddy's knee and feeling his strong arms around you.

FATHER'S DAY

Father's Day has always been special to me because it was the day when, as a baby, I was dedicated to the Lord. I don't remember the event, of course, but it was recounted to me many times growing up, along with other family stories that were told over and over. The message I took to heart was that I was a precious daughter who was wanted, loved and who belonged to the Lord. When it came time for me to personally choose to follow God, my close relationship with my own dad made it that much easier to trust my Heavenly Father with my heart.

As young girls, all of us had tender and sensitive hearts that were easily broken by any disappointment or betrayal. It took time for those wounds to heal and for us to allow ourselves to trust again. You may have even been hurt deeply by your dad or another father figure, causing your view of God as your Heavenly Father to be affected. Whatever our individual past experiences, I'm so glad that there are other ways for us to learn about His character in order to know Him more.

June is such a great time to reflect on nature and the created world around us. Romans 1:20 says, "For since the creation of the world God's invisible qualities – his eternal power and divine nature – have been clearly seen, being understood from what has been made, so that people are without excuse." Have you ever marveled at how a God that made the mountains and wild beasts, in all their enduring, rugged strength, also made the sparrows and lilies, the essence of fragility and tenderness? As women, our hearts were created as tender and fragile so that we would trust Father God as our *Jehovah Jirah*, our provider. A much-quoted passage of Scripture, Matthew 6:25-34, urges us not to worry about tomorrow or be concerned about where our next meal will come from. For as God takes care of the sparrows and lilies, how much more will He provide for those who are created in His image and who trust Him in everything?

We also learn more about our Heavenly Father's character by studying the Bible. Hebrews 12:5-11 in particular gives us an interesting perspective on the spiritual Father-child relationship. As much as we dread the dry, painful seasons of life, the Bible says that they are a necessary part of our growth into true daughters of God. We each need pruning if we ever hope to yield the peaceable fruit of righteousness and reflect our spiritual family resemblance.

We also need to see Father God as a warrior who desires to battle on our behalf. We must learn to cease from trying to fix things – or people – on our own. Our fragile hearts were designed to trust, yield, and obey, and to allow our Father to take the battle for us. Romans 8:37 tells us that we are more than conquerors through Him who loved us. A conqueror is a warrior, so to be more than a conqueror means that we get to reap the rewards of the conquest without having to go to battle. Just as a prince fights a battle in order to take the spoil to the princess he loves, so Jesus has won the battle for us and offers us eternal life free of charge. That's the heart of our Heavenly Father. He longs for you to know Him more so that your trust in Him can be made even more complete. That alone should be reason enough to celebrate Father's Day with tremendous joy and hope as you marvel in the love of your Heavenly Father for you. And if you're like me, and you have always treasured this day, be sure to honour your dad and thank him for doing such a great job at reflecting the Father heart of God. Happy Father's Day!

This week, read Hebrews 12:5-11 and journal your thoughts. Does this align to how you see your Heavenly Father? Ask God to reveal to you circumstances and trials you've experienced that have simply been His loving hand disciplining you. Then ask God to reveal to you battles He has fought on your behalf, and inheritances He has showered on you for simply being his child. Then journal your plans, prayers, feelings, and fears in the shadow of His awesome presence.

RADIANT BEAUTY

Most people hear the word 'model' or 'style' and automatically think of a fashion runway. But if you really think about it, to be a model of something refers to much more than the outward appearance. In a broader sense, it describes a person who is presenting something as an example for others to follow. As women, we are constantly being watched by those around us, many of them hurting from their own past experiences and looking for what might fulfill them. Since it is impossible to have deep conversations with everyone we meet, our outward appearance and dress should reflect what is inside us. That is what I define as a woman's style.

Your style is a very complex and personal attribute, which is influenced by your personality, values, ideals, talents, and sense of self-worth. If asked, many women would say they don't have a style, but they do - they simply haven't taken the time to process who they are, what they have to give, and the manner in which they should give it. Remember, we radiate beauty by *modeling* our style – and as models we are being watched, evaluated, and even emulated by those around us based on our outer appearance. We need to present a positive example to others of what it means to be a beautiful woman living for Jesus in a material, selfish world.

So how does a woman begin to radiate her inner beauty? What does it really mean to be a woman - starting on the inside? First, ponder this: Isn't it amazing how we as women are so different, and yet the same? This apparent paradox tells us something about the mystery of God, and His image that we bear. The image of God is what gives us common features, both physical and spiritual. In this way, we should never feel isolated or alone, because we know we are members of a family: complete with a common heritage, common attributes, and a common future. We also have characteristics that make us unique from anyone else on Earth. You were designed to have a beauty all your own; a crucial, nurturing role to play in this adventure we call life. Once you have a revelation of the identity that we all share in God as well as your specific gifting, then you can begin to radiate your beauty.

Let's be honest, though. It can be a struggle coming to terms with who God made you to be. We all have the same identity in Christ, but God has given each of us different gifts and strengths that we are responsible to cultivate, nurture, and purposefully use for His glory. It's been said that our talents are God's gift to us, but what we do with them is our gift to God. The key is this: being still, resting in His presence, and asking Him to use you to further His kingdom in the way He designed. Being true to yourself and being true to Him were meant to be intertwined, because only by spending time getting to know Him can you truly get to know yourself.

Just as we are created to be unique on the inside, we are also created to be unique on the outside. Like it or not, we must embrace the feeling of being comfortable in our own skin. Women are constantly comparing themselves to each other, which ravages their self-esteem. When you know your new identity through Jesus, and you have recognized the unique gifts He has given you, there should no longer be any reason to compare your looks or talents to another. Yet we still do just that. Why?

Body image is an idol in today's society, and no matter what size we are, we never feel like we measure up. What are the merits to being a size 4 over a size 12? Society never seems to provide a reason, but the message is still loud and clear. Advertising, media, and retail all glorify and cater to the tall, slim woman, leaving all of us in doubt of our true value.

The reason why feeling beautiful is such a craving for women particularly is because we link it with our self-worth. Anti-aging and cosmetic products are in constant demand by women craving to look beautiful so they can feel valuable. If you are a follower of Christ, however, there is good news! You are valued! The Bible says that we were bought with a price – God loved us so much that he sacrificed His only Son in order to pay the ransom for us. This holds true no matter what we look like on the outside, and especially no matter what we look like on the inside. We can come to Him exactly how we are, and He still sees a pearl of great price. I don't know about you, but I find much freedom in reminding myself of this every day.

I love that our Creator, who knows us best, also accepts us just as we are. Our deepest desires for belonging and acceptance are fulfilled through Him. There is no longer any striving to look beautiful to feel valued; we can simply radiate beauty because we *are* valued. It might take a little time, but remember, we are human beings, not human doings. Truly being comfortable in your own skin is about learning to find your contentment in Jesus and realizing all you have, including your beauty, comes from Him. Only the warm fire of His presence flowing through you can dramatically improve your self-esteem and confidence. You will find that even your posture, the way you walk, and how you interact with others will change for the better.

So, if we know our new identity through Jesus, and we've come to terms with who God made us to be, it will follow that we radiate beauty in wonderful new ways. This means that we can showcase our faith before others in a way that is both attractive and genuine. If you visualize a deep well overflowing, you can begin to understand God's heart for you and the kind of woman He wants you to become.

Here's a daily prayer you can put on your dresser mirror or your closet:

> Dear Heavenly Father, as I consider what to wear today, I choose also to clothe myself with modesty. May my manner of dress demonstrate a fulfilled heart that desires only to please You. May my motives, words, actions and reactions be a genuine reflection of the redeeming work you are doing in me. May my appearance, posture and mannerisms enhance, and never detract from, people seeing the real me as a beautiful daughter of the King. I dare to allow my vulnerability and sensitivity to show whenever necessary, because I know You are fighting on my behalf and Your protection is the real covering over my heart and life. I believe You have called me by name and have equipped me with creativity and a beauty of my own to pour out on those around me today. May Your radiance shine through me unhindered as I submit my all to You. In Jesus' Name, Amen.

This week, reflect and journal on what beauty means to you, and your feelings surrounding your personal style. Have your looks ever made you a target of hurtful comments or unwanted attention? Ask God to speak deeply into your heart about the beauty He placed there and write down how he wants you to radiate that beauty.

Plans and Prayers

In your journal, take the time to write out your plans and goals for the coming month of July. Six months on, how are you doing with your New Year's Resolutions? Review them again, asking God to provide what you need to succeed.

How has the Father's heart touched you this month?

Journal the ways you see yourself as being beautiful, or how you want to be more of a Daddy's Girl. In what ways do you model your unique style for His glory? How might you be more intentional in this?

What concerns are on your heart today that you need to write out as prayer requests to God? What answers to prayer can you thank Him for?

Feelings and Fears

What are you feeling today? Joyful? Burdened? Angry? Numb?

Growing up, how did your dad make you feel? Did his affirmations cause you to bloom or was your growth stunted by hurtful words and actions?

Write out how you feel before God, allowing His Father's heart to comfort and affirm your soul and spirit.

What are you concerned about today? Remember, beauty has no worry warts.

Freely journal about whatever comes to mind, as an act of surrendering it all to Him.

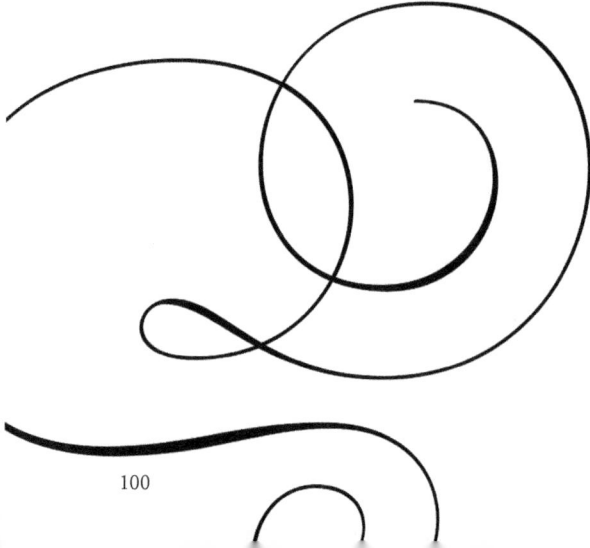

July

The Alabaster Box

There is a familiar story in the Bible of a sinful woman who broke her alabaster box at Jesus' feet. It's found in Luke 7:37-38: "A woman in [the Pharisee's] town who lived a sinful life learned that Jesus was eating at the Pharisee's house, so she came there with an alabaster jar of perfume. As she stood behind him at his feet weeping, she began to wet his feet with her tears. Then she wiped them with her hair, kissed them and poured perfume on them." I was reading a book the other day that made reference to this story and I started to deeply ponder its meaning.

First of all, it's a dialogue without words. It's so true that actions speak louder than words; they are what truly reveal the state of our hearts. And since Jesus knew exactly what was in her heart and what she had done, words were unnecessary - both in her offering of repentance and in her receiving of forgiveness. But her tearful offering was more than that - it cost her something as well. Hers was a sacrificial offering - she broke her alabaster box.

Apparently, in the culture of the day, when a young Jewish woman reached the age of availability for marriage, her family would purchase an alabaster box for her and fill it with precious ointment. The size of the box and the value of the ointment would parallel her family's wealth. This alabaster box would be part of her dowry. When a young man came to ask for her in marriage, she would respond by taking the alabaster box and breaking it at his feet. This gesture of anointing his feet showed him honour. This woman was willing to offer Jesus the best and most valuable thing she had in order to honour Him, knowing it was a one-time gesture that couldn't be done again.

What is in your alabaster box? What are the most precious dreams or secrets you cling to that need to be broken and released to Him? It's not enough to simply give Jesus our hearts, we must allow Him to break them irretrievably as a sign of our faith and complete commitment. Only then can He reform them into what He longs for them to be. Isaiah 55:8 says, "'For My thoughts are not your thoughts, neither are your ways My ways,' declares the Lord. 'As the heavens are higher than the earth, so are my ways higher than your ways and my thoughts than your thoughts.'" God's plans for our lives are so much greater than those we plan for ourselves. Our sacrifice may seem great, but the step of faith He requires to answer His call will always be worth it.

Something else happened when the alabaster box was broken - the fragrance of the oil was released and filled the room. The other people present experienced the aroma and were affected by her very vulnerable, intimate offering. When you begin to live every day by faith, other people will be touched; stirred; challenged; even offended. In fact, those who witnessed this event were appalled and totally misunderstood its meaning. But this woman had come to a place where she no longer cared what people thought of her. It makes no difference what people's reactions are, only that there is something undeniable about you that they will notice. Allow the Holy Spirit to work on their hearts as you remain faithful to His plan and His call. The box is broken, the decision made. There's no turning back now.

This week, posture yourself at Jesus' feet while reading this story again. What are you most fearful of yielding completely to Him? As you journal, commit your fears to paper, and your plans to His sovereign ways.

LIVING THE IMAGE

One of my favourite hobbies is photography; the challenge of capturing a moment in just the right way really appeals to me. It really is true that a picture is worth a thousand words, since images often articulate what mere verbal or written descriptions fail to achieve.

The Bible says that God created us in His image in Genesis 1:27. I don't know about you, but I find this fascinating. No matter what happens in life, or how I feel, I know I possess a kinship with my Creator that can never be taken away! Just as pictures intentionally taken to capture meaningful moments in time, we are designed to purposefully reflect unique aspects of our Creator. Our great God, our Source, our Photographer, composes each of us in a different angle, light, and focus in order to reveal something different about Himself. Amazing!

Here are a few thoughts I had about images:

- Images need angles. Isn't it true that by changing the angle of the camera towards the object, the whole picture can change? The holiness of God required a payment to be made for our sin, and Jesus' death paid that debt in full. Now "we have been made holy through the sacrifice of the body of Jesus Christ once for all" (Hebrews 10:10). We can live in communion with God because God now sees us through the *angle of the cross*. Because of His grace, our own perspective of ourselves and the world is dramatically changed, too!

- Images need light. You can't have a picture without it. The interaction of light and its resulting shadow gives a photo its depth. Matthew 5:14, 16 says, "You are the light of the world. A town built on a hill cannot be hidden. In the same way, let your light shine before others, that they may see your good deeds and glorify your Father in heaven." We all go through times of darkness and doubt, so it's important to remember our light Source. Only then can the tough times act like a shadow, giving our lives depth of character.

- Images need a focus. The most creative photos are composed with some of the picture out of focus, and one object in focus. The effect is incredible as the Photographer clearly defines what He wants the picture to be about. We all know the importance of faith and trusting God when situations seem blurry. In fact the Bible says that "without faith it is impossible to please God" (Hebrews 11:6). If we can learn to appreciate the fuzzy parts of life that require the most faith to walk though, then we will be blown away as we behold the incredible beauty of that Image once it becomes clear. We simply need to focus on Him.

Since becoming an amateur photographer, the biggest challenge for me is trying to capture a moving object. It's really hard to get a sharp picture unless you have a steady hand and lots of skill. What a good reminder to us that being still will reveal more of God's image in us than being busy. We all have times when we need to be busy, but too much speaks 'look at me, see what I can do', while stillness says 'Look at Him, see His image in me.'

This week, take time to be still, allowing the focus of His image inside you to sharpen. Return your eyes to His gaze, your only true light source, and let His light fill you up again. As you journal your plans, prayers, feelings, and fears, describe how it feels to reflect His image and light to the world.

Babies Change Everything

July 22nd marks the birthday of England's newest heir to the throne, Prince George of Cambridge. His arrival in 2013 was heralded by commemorative coins and gun salutes, and the world now eagerly awaits the day he will become King of England. My family had an addition of its own that summer, as well - my sister had a baby girl. Despite the obvious differences between these two, both began by having the same effect on their respective families. Amidst sleepless nights and altered routines, they have brought tremendous hope and joy to these two sets of families that could only be imagined before. It reminds me of the verse I Corinthians 13:12 – For now we see only a reflection as in a mirror; then we shall see face to face. Now I know in part; then I shall know fully, even as I am fully known." Ultrasound pictures give only a dim picture at best of the new life that's about to come into the world, but that just gives that first face-to-face experience a fire all its own.

The fuel for the fire, of course, is the painful labour endured by the mother directly before the miracle comes forth. Are you in a season of labour right now, longing for the birth of a miracle? Just as with the birth of a baby, we don't know when the labour will start, when it will end, or how long it will endure. We can try to plan and prepare in our own strength, but it is God who brings the miracle in His time, and with no guarantees for an easy delivery. However, He does promise us that the joy of the miracle will completely overshadow the pain of the labour that preceded it: "A woman, when she is in labor, has sorrow because her hour has come; but as soon as she has given birth to the child, she no longer remembers the anguish, for joy that a human being has been born into the world. Therefore you now have sorrow; but I will see you again and your heart will rejoice, and your joy no one will take from you." (John 16:21-22)

We must also remember that when our miracle 'baby' comes forth, it is just the beginning. We must dedicate it back to God. Babies grow to influence other people and have babies of their own. So whatever your dream is, when it arrives, don't hold on to it too tightly. Release it back to God and allow Him to use it for His glory and the extension of His kingdom. After all, the birth of Prince George can barely hold a candle to the One born some 2000 years ago. His was heralded by songs of brilliant angels that filled the night sky, and we know that His dominion will be from sea to sea and of His kingdom there will be no end.

This week, journal about your experiences with childbirth, if you've had them. In what ways did they parallel John 16:21-22? If you've never given birth, reflect on how you see the trials of this life being like a woman in labour, with meeting Jesus in heaven as the reward.

Family Generations

Summer is all about community. People are finally free to venture outside of their homes and schedules and spend time doing things together. I was blessed to be able to attend a much-anticipated family reunion recently. We had four generations present, and the majority of us are serving the Lord. We owe our spiritual heritage to my great-grandfather, who had been a bootlegger during the Prohibition Era. Had he not decided to turn his life over to Jesus, we would certainly not be the people we are today. Because of that one life that was transformed by the power of God, entire generations have been nurtured and fruitful in the faith.

Have you ever thought about how your actions and decisions affect other people? What about the effect your life will have on the generations that follow you? The enemy loves to try to isolate people and cause them to think that their attitudes and decisions only concern them. We need to make an active choice to fight for what is good, if simply for the sake of those who will come after us. Deuteronomy 6:7 commands us to teach and train our children diligently; to "talk of [His laws] when you sit at home and when you walk along the road, when you lie down and when you get up." Don't leave the task of biblical instruction to the Sunday School teachers at your church, but engage your children in meaningful conversations about God, His creation, and why being a Christian really is the best way to live. When the disciples kept the children from coming to Jesus, he rebuked them, telling them never to hinder children from coming to Him. The same challenge can be directed at us adults, who may have succumbed long ago to the complacent status quo of daily living. Are we allowing the worries and disappointments of our lives to quench the spark of faith in a child? Children will follow the behaviours they see much more readily than the rules they are given. So, live out what you believe with honesty and integrity, knowing that you are shaping hearts for the future.

It shouldn't stop there, however. There is also a work the Lord wants to do in each of us through the example of children. In Matthew 18:3 Jesus says, "Truly I tell you, unless you change and become like little children, you will never enter the kingdom of heaven." Not only should we be careful instructors of our children, but also humble pupils at times. Their childlike faith should continually revive in us a sense of wonder and renewed trust in Him. He is our Father, Provider, and Healer, so what have we to fear? We are the children that He delights in! So, allow yourself to be filled with a renewed sense of awe and gratitude at the beauty that surrounds you, and let God take care of the rest. Your children will take notice, and only God knows the spiritual impact that will have on generations to come.

And there's more. Hebrews 12:1 tells us that we are currently surrounded by a great cloud of witnesses; those who have gone before us in the faith and are now cheering us on to victory. I picture my great-grandfather there, beaming with pride, joining his voice in with the others. Much of what wasn't realized during their lifetime is being realized by us today, and so the crowd's cheer swells. The finish line is approaching, and I want to finish well. Have an awesome summer!

This week, ask God to give you eyes to see the children around you from His perspective. Also, ask Him to remind you of the saints in heaven – those you know and those you don't – whose faith through the centuries allowed the gospel to reach your ears. As you journal your plans, prayers, feelings and fears, write out intentional prayers for those closest to you that the spiritual potential in their hearts will be cultivated and released more and more each day, to the benefit of others now and long into the future.

Intimacy & Identity

Everyone has heard of Catherine, the modern-day Cinderella Princess. She was born plain Catherine Middleton, but now she is known as Her Royal Highness the Duchess of Cambridge. She did nothing to earn or deserve this change in identity, it was simply offered to her free of charge. The reason? Love. The intimate, committed love from her prince charming, Prince William. We are all enchanted by happily-ever-after princess fairy tales because they awaken in us two powerful longings: Intimacy and Identity. We dream of a handsome prince coming to carry us off on a white horse to his castle in the clouds, where he'll make us his princess and commit to loving us forever … sigh … then the vision ends and the glowing feeling gradually fades as we return to our to-do lists and daily routines. If only we were each destined to be Catherines …

Jesus, your Prince of Peace, wants to do just that. He simply asks that you make yourself vulnerable, like a little child, tearing down all those walls and fronts you use to keep from getting hurt. It's like your heart is homeless before meeting Jesus. It is living on the street and feeling the need to strive and build a makeshift shelter around it with old boxes. However, Prince Jesus now offers your heart a home – a royal palace – where it will finally feel safe and have room to flourish. But first you must tear down the boxes that have been the only comfort you have known. You're still scared of getting hurt; scared of being exposed, embarrassed, and ridiculed. Don't be. He already knows all your hurts and fears, and He will never leave you or betray you. By simply trusting Him with your heart, you can move into his palace of love, forgiveness and acceptance that you only ever dreamed about. In time you will reclaim your vulnerability and willingness to trust, and learn how to lay down your own agenda in favour of His. Only then will you begin to experience the intimacy and identity of a royal princess.

And now, just like Queen Esther, you have been appointed by King Jesus to royal status for such a time as this. Without earning or being deserving of it, King Jesus offers you princess status, a place of belonging, and an invitation to know and be known by Him. This new intimacy and identity is from a kingdom not of this world, but one supernaturally given through the Holy Spirit.

Imagine with me for a moment. You are walking in a meadow on a beautiful spring day, and suddenly a graceful white dove lands gently on your shoulder. What would you do? How would you act? Would you gasp with wonder, and want to linger in the moment? Would you stand up straighter, and put on a gentler demeanor so as not to scare it away? Stay in that thought for a moment, for the Bible describes the Holy Spirit as a dove. Pure and holy, He lives inside every believer, but never forces His way in. He can even be silenced, quenched, and dismissed. To quote Rev. Bill Johnson, "There's a dove on your shoulder – walk with the dove in mind."

Being a princess in love with a prince is a lot like walking with a dove on your shoulder. It exhilarates you initially but requires special care and wisdom to maintain that emotional state over time. Some days may even feel mundane, and crises will still arise. But all the more reason why you need to learn to "walk in a manner worthy of the calling you have received" (Ephesians 4:1b). You may not always feel the transcendent splendour you felt when the dove first came to you, but He's there. With His guidance, you can:

- Be dignified with gentleness – standing up straight, free of shame, behaving graciously
- Be confident with humbleness – holding up your head, walking in awe of what you carry
- Be self-aware with selflessness – sensing His touch, seeking to show it to others
- Be regal with kindness - embracing your high position, living to bestow it on others

Now that your position has been established, you need to learn about the old French expression called *'noblesse oblige'*. It simply means that those who have noble status should act nobly and give generously to those in need. Queen Esther used her royal status to courageously save her people: what is God calling you to do with yours? Remember, this royal status wasn't given to you to simply secure your place in heaven, but to give you a king's ransom in resources to serve those around you. But don't be overwhelmed. As the collective Bride of Christ, we work best together, encouraging each other and praying for one another. The Apostle Paul exhorts in Colossians 1:9-10, "For this reason we also, since the day we heard it, do not cease to pray for you, and to ask that you may be filled with the knowledge of His will in all wisdom and spiritual understanding; that you may have a *walk worthy* of the Lord, fully pleasing Him, being fruitful in every good work and increasing in the knowledge of God." You don't have to do this alone, my friend!

Remember Catherine, now the Duchess of Cambridge? As amazing as her transformed identity is, she can hope for even greater things. She is in line to one day become a princess, and then a queen. We can have hope of more, too! As great as being a princess-in-waiting is, complete with white dove perfectly poised, we also have hope of spending eternity with Jesus, our bridegroom, in that castle in the clouds! One day, when you least expect it, He will come for you and carry you off with him to the sky! It doesn't get any better than that!

This week, reflect on the idea of having a dove on your shoulder, journaling how you would feel, what you would do, and where you would go. As you pray, reflect on what *noblesse oblige* means to you, as a royal princess possessing limitless power and resources before a world in need.

Plans and Prayers

In your journal, take the time to write out your plans and goals for the coming month of August.

What do you love about summer? What do you not like?

In what ways can your summer more intentionally celebrate the people God has placed around you?

Write out some practical ways in which you could minister to a neighbour, invite someone to your church, over for a meal, or connect with a long-lost relative.

With the limitless resources at hand through prayer, how will you bless others today? How does your royal status affect how you pray?

What things do you need to confess to Him? Thank Him for?

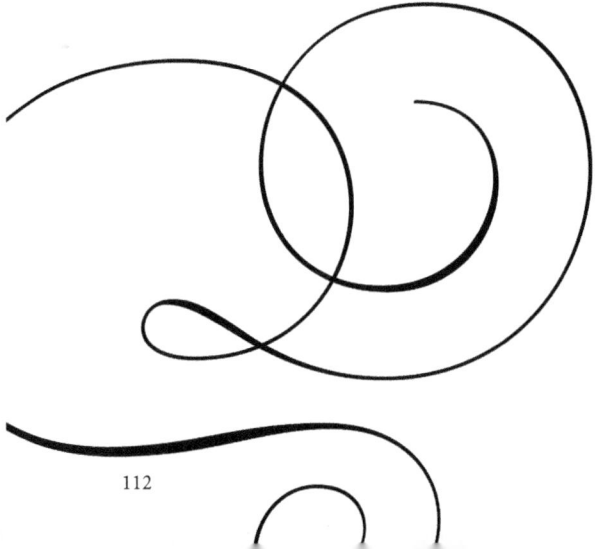

Feelings and Fears

What are you feeling today? Joyful? Burdened? Frustrated? Numb?

What boxes surround your heart that you need to tear down?

Write out how you feel before God. He's offering your heart a palace and your head a crown if you will trust him with everything.

What are you concerned about today?

Freely journal about whatever comes to mind, as an act of surrendering it all to Him.

August

The Hidden Treasure

I recently had the experience of selling my home. It took a lot of preparation as well as patience; an interesting combination of ownership of the situation and a surrendered release of control. First, there was the task of improving and maintaining my home as a perfectly clean and staged environment to attract as many potential buyers as possible. Next, I was required to interact with strangers in a manner that was both warm and friendly as well as reserved and professional. As difficult as these tasks were, I also knew I needed to continually give the matter entirely over to the Lord and allow Him free reign to provide His best for me. I knew I was not to take the success or failure of my best efforts to heart, as it would ultimately be the Lord's doing according to His plan. As I was single, the process also struck me as being very similar to another major season of life for a woman: that of finding a husband. Seeking a buyer for your home is a lot like a woman desiring marriage; there are many things you can do to prepare yourself, but the ultimate result is in the Lord's hands.

First of all, it's paramount to remember that it's the man's job to seek after a wife, not the other way around. Proverbs 18:22 says "he who finds a wife finds what is good and receives favour from the Lord." Each of us women are treasures to be found; hidden gems that need to behave as such to be truly valued by the seeker. Everyone loves looking for buried treasure; the adventure of the hunt and the thrill of discovery are as rewarding as the treasure itself. If you are single, ask the Lord how He best wants you to position yourself to be found by the man He has for you. I love the verse in Proverbs 4:23 that says "above all else, guard your heart, for everything you do flows from it." Your heart, which contains your deepest feelings, convictions, and motives, is the source of your personality and your inner beauty, and what makes you a treasure worth discovering. If you don't choose to keep it hidden in Christ and allow Him to bring just the right seeker along in His time, you will likely endure suffering, grief, regret, and other consequences that will clutter your future life. You need to continually remind yourself that it's the man who seeks, the woman who responds, and the Lord who orchestrates the entire process from beginning to end.

So how exactly do you prepare yourself for receiving God's best? Think of how you would prepare your home before putting it on the market.

- Do some market research. What are your precise reasons for desiring marriage, and what specific qualities are you looking for in a husband? There are many excellent books on marriage out there that detail what being a wife really means. For example, are you prepared and willing to respect, trust, and serve your husband? All three of these responsibilities are keys to a husband's well-being and the maintenance of a happy and peaceful household. Ask God to purify your desires, prepare you to serve, and keep your heart the hidden oasis that it was meant to be.

- Seek advice, opinions, and wise counsel. Women are not called to exist in isolation, but in community. Prayerfully seek out the wisdom of women who are in happy marriages and stay accountable to them. They have had experiences you can benefit from and can offer insight and support along the way.

- Be prepared to make an investment. Like a home refurbishing, preparing your heart for marriage requires time, money, energy, perseverance, humility and obedience. We owe it to the Holy Spirit, our heart's owner and inhabitant, to invest what we have towards managing our inner world well during such a delicate and personal process.

- Consider the curb appeal. Does your outward appearance say what you want it to say? Do you need to work on your complexion, your diet, or your wardrobe? Don't be afraid to get a close friend's honest opinion, and humbly and prayerfully proceed one step at a time. The most important thing to remember is to be yourself, and working on your curb appeal is simply about learning how to let the best parts of you shine!

- Address the lighting and the colours. Once a potential buyer shows interest, they will want to see the inside. Are there corners or places in your heart that have shadows of doubt, fear, unforgiveness, or pride? The best way to liven up a dull room is to brighten it with better light and colour. Bring yourself into the Light and surrender all to the Holy Spirit's work.

- Pray for the buyer. While you're preparing your own heart, pray that God prepares his, too. Pray that your future husband begins to learn even now how to love you sacrificially as Christ loved the church. Pray that he resists temptation and channels his desires into wholesome, life-giving pursuits. Pray for strong friendships and accountability relationships to strengthen his character and prepare him for marriage.

When an offer to purchase is made on a home, there will likely be some negotiations needed from both parties in order to finalize the contract. Whether it's the price, the inclusions, or the possession date, neither party will have their ideal scenario presented. Compromise is essential to mutually satisfy. The same goes with entering a marriage; you need to be willing to discuss minor things openly, honestly and not defensively. By reminding yourself that your heart is hidden in Christ, you will be more willing to discuss these things without harboring ill-feeling when disagreements arise. You will also be better positioned to allow the Lord to remain in control.

What if your house is on the market for longer than you expected? Would that cause you to feel desperate and consider lowering the price? Another important attribute you must value is integrity, ensuring your identity and self-worth are unshakably rooted in Christ. As women, our greatest fear is feeling alone or unwanted. When the years start to pass by and you haven't met Mr. Right, it can seem tempting to lower your standards and settle for someone you know isn't the one for you just to gain the security. My house was on the market much longer than I anticipated, and I was certainly tempted to take a desperate course of action. But after much prayer, the Lord gave me the strength and will to hold on, and it was worth it.

So, what happened with my home sale? Despite the fact that I was attempting to sell during a very competitive season, the Lord provided a buyer at the last moment. God delights in coming through for His children, particularly in dramatic ways! I can therefore be assured and confident that He will provide a husband for me as well; in His own time, and in His own way.

This week, reflect on how you interact with your husband (or with men). Do you desire their attention more than God's? Journal honestly about what you feel it means to be a hidden treasure, and to have a heart hidden in Christ. If you are single and seeking a husband, write down some steps you could take to navigate this season with wisdom and integrity. Then pray for your husband and for the single men you know that they would seek God first in all they pursue.

LIFE AT THE ALTAR

Have you ever heard stories of women who were 'left at the altar'? Their wedding day dawned, they arrived at the church full of dreams, and the groom failed to show up! How devastating! We instinctively feel their pain deeply, because rejection is a woman's greatest fear. The heart of a woman continually asks, 'Am I wanted? Am I desired? Am I loved?' Receiving no response is discouraging, but receiving a negative reply deflates her entire world. All women have experienced rejection in some form at some time, whether by a man, a parent, or a friend. We cry, we feel hurt, we feel angry, and we will do anything to make the pain go away. Yet God wants to meet us in those moments – as our lover, father, and best friend – and draw us closer to Himself. He promises to never leave us or reject us. Never ever. (Deut. 31:8)

As painful as it is to be left at the altar, remember what the altar means.

Many young women make it their goal in life to 'get a man to the altar' before they turn thirty. Whether bewitched by romantic fairy-tale stories or a desire to pacify a void in their life, waiting for God's choice and timing is dismissed as an option. Many become skilled at manipulation, flirtation, and compromise, not realizing Whose they really are or the greater purpose He has called them to. Still others are consumed by lust, fear, or pride, propelling them to find a husband early and make marriage the answer to everything. To so many women, the altar symbolizes fulfillment, happiness, and dreams coming true. In short, it becomes an idol. Yet when rejection and disillusionment come, whether before or after the wedding day, the idol is torn down, bringing identity and self-worth down along with it.

Whether that is a major part of your story or not, the false idol of the altar has likely deceived you to some degree. Perhaps it was a childhood dream that was shattered, or a longing for romance gone unanswered. And yet right there, where you're lying at the foot of the broken altar you'd built, Jesus meets you. He reveals to you *where* you really are, in front of the glorious altar of His presence, and *who* you really are, his beautiful and beloved bride. Slowly and tenderly, He lifts you to your feet, offering you an invitation to find out what an altar really is and what your life is really meant to be about.

An altar was originally a place of sacrifice. In Old Testament times, the altar was where the animal sacrifices occurred. It was bloody, messy, and costly. Animals gave their lives and shed their blood to atone for the sins of their owners; animals that could otherwise have been sold or used for food and clothing. In 1 Chronicles 21:18-26, we read the story of David building an altar to God in order to stop a plague from coming upon Jerusalem. Because he was the King, the owner of the land offered to give David the altar site free of charge. Yet David refused, saying "I will not take for the Lord what is yours, nor sacrifice a burnt offering that costs me nothing." Approaching the altar is costly in every way.

In being a place of costly sacrifice, the altar was also a place of worship. Even costly sacrifice can be done in a self-seeking ritual fashion, but worship requires engagement of heart and soul. The Apostle Paul urges in Romans 12:1 to "offer your bodies as a living sacrifice, holy and pleasing to God – this is your true and proper worship." Though Jesus' death on the cross freed us from the necessity of animal sacrifice for our atonement, the altar still remains, calling us to sacrifice every part of our being to Him in heartfelt worship.

Finally, we must not forget that the altar is a place of invitation. It was God himself who made you, loved you, and drew you closer to His presence at the altar. Jesus paid the ultimate sacrifice so that our relationship could be restored to God the Father. He delights in us, in our worship, and in meeting our need for intimacy and identity that we thought only a man could fill. In fact, Hebrews 4:16 says, "Let us approach our merciful God with confidence, so we may receive grace just when we need it." No longer are we laying as broken vessels at his feet, but now invited to stand tall in his presence, locked in His gaze, robed in white.

And the altar's symbolism goes on. It is also a place of protection, consecration, testimony and covenant-making. Church buildings continue to be constructed with the altar as the focus. It is a very public place. God longs to be worshipped and celebrated by all tribes and nations, and to be found by all who seek Him. Wedding ceremonies centre around the altar as a public symbol of God's participation in the marriage covenant, and of His delight in the couple's vows of commitment to each other.

The altar is all of these things when God is at the centre. But when we reduce the altar to anything human-centric, we are doomed to have it crumble at some point. Yet God's grace is so abundant and His love so vast, that He will meet you there - and give you such a sense of completion and purpose that it will exceed your wildest dreams!

I love the story of the woman at the well in John 4. Unnamed and a Samaritan by birth, she is the epitome of a rejected woman in Palestinian culture. In that day, women had no rights and no property, so they depended on having a husband or male relative to support and protect them. When we learn that this woman had five husbands, we assume today that she must have been dissatisfied with them or unfaithful to them. But in light of her cultural and economic need for a husband, this seems unlikely. Because women had no rights, men in that day could get away with divorcing their wives on almost any ground: if she couldn't cook, talked too much, was barren, or failed to live up to Proverbs 31 in some way. And this poor woman endured such rejection *five times*! Talk about being left at the altar! So now, desperate for support and protection, she has chosen to live with someone who won't even take her to the altar. Shunned by her community and filled with shame, she goes to the well alone – and meets Jesus! He sees her pain and begins teaching her about worship! The well immediately becomes the altar she has longed for all her life, and Jesus her source of true fulfillment. No other discourse in the Gospels is as lengthy or as deep as this initial conversation between Jesus and this unnamed woman. Jesus, in his humanity, knew rejection and loneliness well, and empathized with rejected and lonely individuals more than with others. This is wonderful news for us women who have experienced rejection and loneliness at some time, to recognize the soft spot Jesus has for us in His heart and in His kingdom.

Have you ever reflected on all the limitations Jesus took on when He came to Earth to save us? Time, space, physical flesh, and *gender*. As a single man, he would have felt the same loneliness that most single adults feel, and yet he knew that his mission on Earth did not include marriage. The disciples he poured into for three years all deserted him at his death, leaving the deepest ache of rejection and loneliness. Yet Jesus knew his identity, purpose, and calling and had perfect unity and intimacy with the Father and the Holy Spirit, which gave him the courage to persevere and obey. So as the popular worship song says, come to the altar. Jesus is calling.

This week, visit the altar at your church, and reflect on everything it symbolizes to you. How has our culture made it more about weddings than about His presence? Journal freely to Him all the rejection, fear, and loneliness you carry, knowing how fully He understands and longs to lift you up. Then meet Him at the altar again, fully surrendered to His plans, and let him clothe you in white.

The Hope Chest

What do you hope for? Have you given up hope about something, or feel pressure to resign yourself to being okay with the way things are? As Christians, we're often misled into believing that all longing and desire is wrong, and that contentment and satisfaction are what define holiness. Yes, it is true that our hearts can be deceitful and our desires have selfish roots, but there still exists righteous longing just like there exists righteous anger. The mark of a mature Christian is one who is led by a different Spirit – the Holy Spirit – to seek and desire what God desires.

You may be familiar with something called a hope chest. Also called a dowry chest, trousseau chest, or glory box, it is a decorative piece of storage furniture that a teenage girl would traditionally use to store linens, bedding, heirlooms, and clothing for future use during her wedding and marriage. Often handed down from mother to daughter, hope chests connected generations of women in a family together, as each new owner replenished and renewed the contents and the hope. Far from being purely utilitarian, hope chests were often richly decorated, carved, and painted. Many were made of cedar because of its moth-repelling properties. In other words, they were made to last; to encapsulate legacies and dreams for generations. When a mother bestowed her hope chest upon her eldest daughter, the momentous symbolism it carried was to expand a girl's expectations for the future; to envision her own daughters and granddaughters, and ultimately eternity.

Hope is a powerful thing – and Scripture instructs us where and how to direct our hope in order to stir up, and not grieve, the Holy Spirit within us. Our flesh longs for immediate, physical gratification, whereas the Holy Spirit longs for what is eternal, spiritual, and lasting. Romans 8:24-25 states, "For in this hope we were saved. But hope that is seen is no hope at all. Who hopes for what they already have? But if we hope for what we do not yet have, we wait for it patiently." The difference, therefore, between selfish longing and righteous longing is the effect on our character. Selfish longing makes us anxious, where righteous longing grows our patience. Proverbs 13:12 observes, "Hope deferred makes the heart sick, but a longing fulfilled is a tree of life." The wisdom of Proverbs is in its keen observation of human nature, recognizing here and warning against conceiving desire for what is not guaranteed. Indeed, everything that we hope for in this life could be put in this category, making righteous longing the only hope we have that is truly assured.

Like the contents of a hope chest, which materially symbolize assurance of the life to come, we have been given a taste of glory through the Holy Spirit living inside of us. His presence is designed to secure our faith, remind us of our true identity, and give our hearts wings to long for more. Psalm 130:5 declares, "I wait for the Lord, my whole being waits, and in His Word I put my hope." Even when things are going well, there is still something wondrous and transcendent about remembering that this is only a taste of the glory that will be revealed to us in heaven. There we will know the true meaning of home and belonging, which are definitely things worth hoping for!

This righteous hope, though, is not a passive thing; it is a hope that should mobilize you to action. Romans 12:11-12 commands: "Do not let your zeal subside; keep your spiritual fervour, serving the Lord. Be joyful in hope, patient in affliction, faithful in prayer." Like a young girl awaiting her wedding day, there is much preparation to be done and many treasures to be gathered for the hope chest before the day arrives. Jesus says, "Do not store up for yourselves treasures on earth, but treasures in heaven. For where your treasure is, there your heart will be also" (Matthew 6:19-21). Jesus is warning that efforts made to attain earthly treasures never bring lasting reward, and in so doing one risks their very heart. But efforts made towards heavenly treasures reveal a heart of wisdom, because they will yield an incorruptible prize. So ponder this: what does your heavenly hope chest contain? Testimonies of people you have mentored or led to the Lord? Sacrifices you have made for His Kingdom? Ministries you have joyfully served and supported? Prayers you have faithfully offered without receiving immediate results? If so, you should picture each as a beautiful garment or embroidered tapestry carefully placed in an elaborate hope chest in heaven engraved with your name. Nothing will ever compare to it on earth, so why be anxious another moment? Though this life never promises to be an easy road, you can experience supernatural peace and joy along the way as you work diligently for His kingdom, allowing your spirit to long and hope for the day when it will finally be joined in marriage to Jesus. As you prepare for your heavenly wedding, remember: "If you keep yourself pure, you will be a special vessel for honourable use, set apart as holy, useful to the Master, and prepared for every good work" (2 Timothy 2:21). Happy Wedding Day!

This week, imagine and design your heavenly hope chest. What treasures would it contain? What precious jewels and spotless linens would compose your wedding trousseau? Write a love letter to Jesus, as a besotted fiancée would write to her beloved far away. Allow a righteous longing and hope from the Holy Spirit fill you up to overflowing as you journal.

The Bridegroom is Coming

The Parable of the Ten Virgins, in Matthew 25:1-13, often seems like an antiquated and romanticized fairy tale, oddly-placed within Jesus' apocalyptic description of the end times. Yet when explored deeper, both its meaning and placement correlate perfectly with Jesus' mission and message. I always knew there was great marriage symbolism throughout Jesus' teaching, so recently I decided to look into learning more about first century Jewish weddings and what Jesus' original Jewish audience would have understood from this parable.

First of all, there was the betrothal. A prospective bridegroom would go to the home of his chosen bride and give her a gift that signified his commitment and love for her, as a promise toward their upcoming union as husband and wife. Once she accepted his gift, the pair were then legally married, though not yet allowed to live together. Immediately following the betrothal was a necessary period of separation for preparation. The bridegroom would be busy preparing a place for them to live, usually by building an additional room on his father's house. The bride was also busy preparing her wedding garments and keeping herself ready for his unannounced return. The bridegroom's return would usually be at night, and always a surprise. Only the bridegroom's father would know the exact moment, since it was he who would give the final approval for the bridegroom to retrieve his bride and for the lavish wedding feast to begin. In ancient Jewish times, the wedding feast would last seven days and consist of food, wine, music, dancing and celebration. If the bride wasn't ready or if she was discovered to be impure in some way, there would be great shame and loss.

Jesus is the Bridegroom, and we, as His Church, are the bride. He has said, "I will betroth you to me forever; I will betroth you in righteousness and justice, in love and compassion. I will betroth you in faithfulness, and you will acknowledge the Lord" (Hosea 2:19-20). The seal and promise of our betrothal is the Holy Spirit, which Jesus has given to us: "And I will ask the Father, and he will give you another advocate to help you and be with you forever – the Spirit of truth" (John 14:16-17). His love through the Holy Spirit is to be "like a seal over your heart, like a seal on your arm; for love is as strong as death, its jealousy unyielding as the grave. It burns like blazing fire, like a mighty flame. Many waters cannot quench love; rivers cannot sweep it away" (Song of Solomon 8:6-7). Though we must now endure a painful period of separation, Jesus has left us with these words: "Do not let your hearts be troubled. You believe in God; believe also in me. My Father's house has many rooms; if that were not so, would I have told you that I am going there to prepare a place for you? And if I go and prepare a place for you, I will come back and take you to be with me that you also may be where I am" (John 14:1-3). So as His chosen bride, we must make ourselves ready, preparing ourselves for His sudden triumphant return. "For the Lord Himself will come down from heaven, with a loud command, with the voice of the archangel and with the trumpet call of God […] and we will meet the Lord in the air" (I Thessalonians 4:16,17). The waiting will be over, and the celebrations will begin. Revelation 19:7-8,9 says, "Let us rejoice and be glad and give him glory! For the wedding of the Lamb has come, and his bride has made herself ready. Fine linen, bright and clean, was given her to wear […] blessed are those who are invited to the wedding supper of the Lamb!"

With the backdrop now painted, we can now move to examining the Parable of the Ten Virgins itself. A week of wedding festivities is about to culminate in the bridegroom's torched processional with his guests through the town to enter the final feast. Ten virgin maidens wait impatiently with the bride in her home, but only five are wise enough to bring extra oil for their torches. As night falls, the bridesmaids grow weary in their waiting and fall asleep, letting their torches burn out. At midnight, they wake to hear the procession call out, "Here's the bridegroom!" The five who are wise are able to light their torches again and join in, while the foolish five are unprepared, and ultimately excluded from the feast.

The most unusual characteristic of this parable is, of course, the refusal of the bridegroom to allow the foolish virgins to enter the feast late. We would expect that after such a joyful and public processional, all the more anticipated because of the bridegroom's long delay, that the delay of a few guests would be overlooked. Yet this shocking twist parallels the negative element of surprise in the other apocalyptic parables, for the surprise return of the Bridegroom will be one of judgment. The wedding feast will only be joyful for those who are prepared when he returns. Matthew is warning his audience that the welcoming door of Jesus will only remain so for a limited time, and to ask themselves, "Could I be one of the foolish virgins?" Only Jesus has the authority to judge people, and even then his mercy is so great as to delay his coming. For he is "not wanting anyone to perish, but everyone to come to repentance" (2 Peter 3:9). All ten virgins had been invited to the wedding and they all knew the bridegroom well enough to recognize him when he came, but only five knew that their invitation came with a demand for both watchfulness and obedience. The foolish virgins wanted to experience the joy and excitement of the wedding without taking the steps necessary to prepare themselves for it. So be ready, for the Bridegroom is coming.

This week, read Matthew 25:1-13 again, picturing yourself as both a wise and a foolish maiden. Ask God to remind you often of the imminence of His return and how he wants you to prepare your heart for it.

THE WEDDING SUPPER

I've always loved going to weddings. I really enjoy studying all the beautiful details and marveling at the planning that went into bringing the event to life. I don't even mind being simply a spectator at a wedding ceremony, but there's a special meaning attached to those instances when I've also been invited to attend the reception. To be personally invited by the bride and groom means I am no longer a spectator but now a participant. My presence matters; there is a place reserved for me at the table. Jesus says in John 14:2 that He is preparing a place for you; a mansion of glory and a seat of honour at the wedding supper of the Lamb. It is sure to be incredibly beautiful and equally thrilling knowing we each have a place to belong and a seat to fill. You see, the beauty inherent in a wedding celebration is only meant to serve as a backdrop; the coming together of two people intimately and permanently is the focus. It's all about relationship. The wedding supper of the Lamb will be focused on Jesus, the Lamb, our Bridegroom, who laid down His life for us, His bride.

It will be a day that not even our wildest imaginations could prepare us for. I remember when I was ten, I was invited to my first wedding reception. My aunt and uncle were married earlier that day, and all their friends and family were now gathered at the reception hall to celebrate their union. I was told to be on my best behaviour and instructed on proper table manners and etiquette. Yet nothing could have prepared me for what was about to happen! The moment came when all the single ladies were called to catch the bride's bouquet, and I made my way to the front of the group. I can still remember my excitement when I watched those little flowers fly through the air and land at my feet, where I quickly picked them up. I remember vividly how thrilled I was to be honoured in such a way, and I kept that bouquet in a vase for years. It symbolized both my participation in and belonging to something greater than myself - a wedding - and an elaborate bestowing of honour and grace from my receiving such an unexpected gift.

This is a picture of what heaven promises to be like. Revelation 19:6-7 says "and I heard, as it were, the voice of a great multitude, as the sound of many waters and as the sound of mighty thunderings, saying 'Alleluia! For the Lord God Omnipotent reigns! Let us be glad and rejoice and give Him glory, for the marriage of the Lamb has come, and His wife has made herself ready.'" As the bride of the Lamb, we were created by our Bridegroom to live a life of continual preparation and ongoing response to the Holy Spirit so that we may be ready when the fullness of time comes. We anticipate and long for that moment, as one waits for an approaching wedding, all the while knowing that our reward in heaven will bestow more honour and glory than we could ever prepare for or imagine.

I don't know about you, but meditating on this truth seems to make all the trials of life worthwhile. I love II Corinthians 4:16-18: "Do not lose heart. Though outwardly we are wasting away, yet inwardly we are being renewed day by day. For our light and momentary troubles are achieving for us an eternal glory that far outweighs them all. So we fix our eyes not on what is seen, but on what is unseen, since what is seen is temporary, but what is unseen is eternal." Just as the deeply emotional and spiritual bond between a bride and groom can only be hinted at tangibly through beautiful flowers and decorations, so it is with our life here as we know it. We catch but glimpses of eternity that can only serve to whet our appetites and deepen our longings for the fulfillment of all that is being prepared for us in Heaven. Amen. Come, Lord Jesus!

This week, journal some memories of weddings you've been in or attended, and your feelings that day. What did it mean to you to have a place at the table, and to belong? How do you anticipate the beautiful unity and splendor of heaven to be like an eternal wedding?

Plans and Prayers

In your journal, take the time to write out your plans and goals for the coming month of September.

How did you grow in your faith this summer?

How have these devotionals about weddings, hope, and preparation brought you closer to your Heavenly Bridegroom?

What concerns are on your heart today that you need to write out as prayer requests to God? What answers to prayer can you thank Him for?

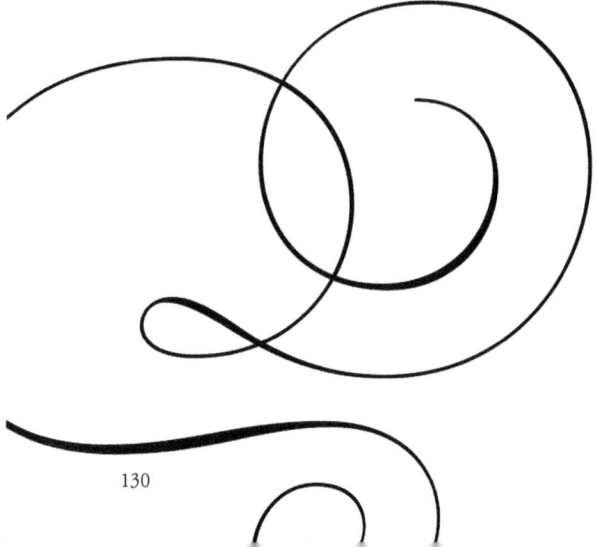

Feelings and Fears

What are you feeling today? Joyful? Burdened? Angry? Numb?

How does waiting for something make you feel?

Write out how you feel before God. He's been in your shoes and knows what you're going through.

What aspects of the coming fall season concern you the most? Bring you the most hope?

Freely journal about whatever comes to mind, as an act of surrendering it all to Him.

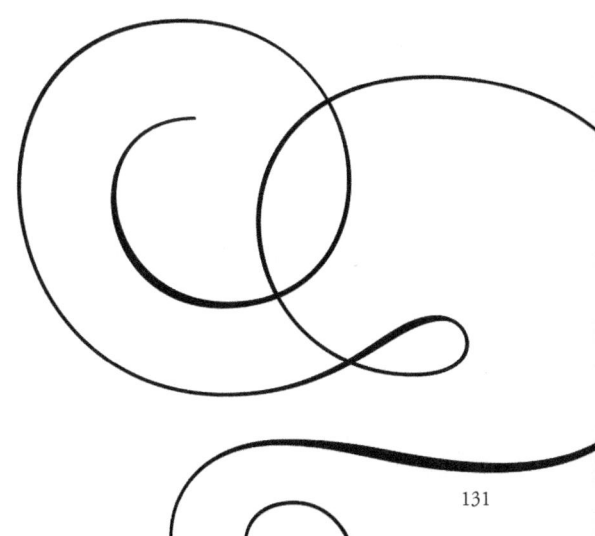

September

Ruth's Redemption

I did an in-depth study once on the book of Ruth, the Bible story about the foreign widow from Moab who gave up everything to devote her life to her mother-in-law Naomi. If you haven't read the story in a while, please do so. It's a short yet beautiful tale of devotion and sacrifice that we all, as women, need to be inspired by on a regular basis. Naomi was an Israelite living in the pagan land of Moab with her husband, two sons, and their Moabite wives. Tragically, all three men died within a short time frame. Destitute and in deep mourning, Naomi decided to go back to Israel where she heard there was food and where she at least had her husband's overgrown land to live on. As an act of kindness, she then offered to release her daughters-in-law from their bond to her through marriage and return to their homes. One girl went home, the other refused. Why? Why did Ruth, as grieved and destitute as the other two, desire to move to a foreign land? The only explanation is that she had met the God of Israel and wanted to serve only Him.

Moabites would have been very familiar with the Israelites and how their God had brought them out of slavery in Egypt, caused them to cross on dry ground through the Red Sea, and then conquer many mighty Canaanite nations in order to settle in their land. Ruth also may have remembered the Israelite victory over Moab itself, which brought peace between them for a while. So it may have been very natural for Ruth to be intrigued by this Israelite refugee family living in her land, particularly their eldest son. Upon her marriage to him, Ruth's desire to know the God of her husband's family only increased.

I can imagine it all started on their wedding night. This tall, handsome man she married with the dark eyes and adorable accent was also *circumcised*. What did that mean? What was it about his family's covenant that made it so uniquely binding? I imagine during those ten years of marriage, Ruth would have participated in Passovers, Holy Festivals, and heard family stories of Yahweh's covenant of love, which stirred her spirit. Even in spite of the fact that Ruth did not bear any children, a tragic crisis in those days, she still embraced the God of Israel as her own.

It was this same tenacity of spirit and determined will that caused Ruth to not only want to stay with Naomi as a help and a comfort to her, but also to declare a solemn vow to serve Naomi's God and allow Him to strike her down if she ever broke her word. What determination! What a sacrifice of loyalty! To make such a solemn vow, Ruth would have had to know a great deal about the Hebrew covenant and the character of God, and perhaps something more. I would even like to go so far as to suggest one particular story of recent Hebrew victory that Ruth may have been told, and been particularly inspired by, to make such a decision.

Before the defeat of Jericho, just one generation prior to this, Joshua had sent two spies into it to peruse the area and its fortification. While at the peril of their lives in this city, a prostitute named Rahab hid them in her house and then lied to the Jericho officials that the spies had left. You see, Rahab had also heard of the mighty hand of the God of Israel and desired for her and her family to be spared when He caused the city to fall. Because of her courage and her desire to serve Yahweh, she and her household were kept safe, and later came to dwell with the Israelites. What's more, Rahab eventually married one of the spies she had hid. I can imagine Ruth's eyes widening as she first heard this story, and perhaps the Lord used this means to plant in her heart the same courage and desire to serve Him.

Such strength of character in Ruth soon became desperately needed once her husband passed away. Though Naomi's grief caused her to become bitter and self-absorbed, Ruth's grief brought out from her deep empathy and devotion. Unsurprisingly, Naomi was shocked and bewildered by Ruth's vow. It's all fine and good to have a companion for the journey; she certainly welcomed that part. But what was she to say to her friends when she arrived back in Bethlehem with this foreign girl? How was she best to look after and provide for her? It was enough for Naomi to try and figure out how she herself was to survive, let alone another person. The Bible says that, after Ruth made her vow, Naomi said no more to her. It leads me to believe that the pair walked the remainder of the journey in silence, both contemplating and preparing themselves as best they could for what the future might bring. I also speculate that

God began to speak to Ruth and fill her with His Spirit during those days of silent pilgrimage; there is no other explanation for the radical feats of strength and courage she performed in the coming weeks.

Upon arrival in Bethlehem, the dreaded reunion between Naomi and her former friends took place. Naomi is completely spent; emotionally, spiritually, and now physically. No wonder she disowned her pleasant-sounding name and espoused the bitter 'Mara' as a more fitting title, for that is exactly how she felt. Ruth, on the other hand, stood by quietly as Naomi voiced her lament anew. I don't think Ruth was offended when Naomi described herself as 'empty'; I'm sure she was filled with compassion once again for her dear mother-in-law who had known three times more the grief and pain than she.

When the next day dawned, Ruth determined to find food for them to eat, even if it meant gleaning in the fields in the hot sun all alone. In Israelite law, field owners were supposed to leave some grain behind during harvest for the poor and the widows, so Ruth went out looking for leftovers. If it had just been herself to worry about, I'm sure she would have been content with that. But her vow to God and Naomi was pressing on her mind; she knew she had to do something more drastic. She found a field whose foreman seemed somewhat approachable, and boldly asked if she could reap instead of glean. What a suggestion! She was obviously a foreigner, not skilled, and unknown to anyone. Yet God gave her favour with him, and she was allowed to reap from the freshly-cut barley sheaves, providing her with much more grain for much less labour. Later that day, God continued to show His favour by bringing the field owner himself to the place where Ruth was working. His name was Boaz, a wealthy landowner, but more importantly, He was a man after God's own heart (like father, like great-grandson, David!). Once the foreman pointed out Ruth to him, he immediately made the connection. He had heard all about her loyal character with regards to Naomi, and, knowing she had no means of provision, freely embraced her as one of his working women and even allowed her to eat at his table. The fact that she was a foreigner meant nothing to him. What favour! What kindness! No wonder Ruth fell prostrate at his feet in reverence and gratitude.

Upon returning to Naomi at the end of the day, Ruth joyfully showed her how much grain she has gathered and offered her some of the food she had kept from the dinner table. What a tremendous overflow of blessing! Naomi, in her bitter state, probably kept telling herself all day not to get her hopes up. She probably visited with her friends again and continued to commiserate along the same lines as yesterday. Yet remember, we serve an awesome God; one so awesome and caring that He will choose to provide abundance despite our lack of expectation. What's more, Ruth told Naomi about meeting the landowner, and finished her story by mentioning his name as if it were an afterthought. Immediately, a spark ignited in Naomi's eyes – eyes that had been dark and lifeless for a long, long time – and she revealed to Ruth that Boaz was a near kinsman to their family. For a family that had been depleted of its immediate male relatives, this news was a very welcome breath of fresh air. Just hearing the word 'family' again must have brought to their minds memories of happier days; of family birthdays, and those familiar Holy Feasts and Passovers. Only God knew this was just the beginning.

The weeks passed, and Ruth continued to reap in Boaz's field under the protection of His other women. Things were looking up. Naomi's grief began to subside, and she began to look outside of herself. Slowly, a burden for Ruth's future formed in her heart. I expect she started praying earnestly for wisdom; once she died, what would become of Ruth? A barren, foreign widow is the last woman any man in Israel would choose to marry, and yet marry she must in order to be provided for in that culture. A plan began to form in Naomi's mind. She knew Boaz to be a close kinsman, and an upstanding man in the community who had shown great favour to Ruth all these weeks. Would he have her? How is the subject even to be brought up, since they had no male spokesperson? Ruth must speak herself, and it must be done in secret.

What followed was a very unorthodox proceeding, but theirs was a very desperate situation. Naomi had her husband's land, but no man to work it and no heir to inherit it. At Naomi's death, it would go to her husband's closest male relative, and Ruth wouldn't even have a place to live. Something had to be done that would both secure the land now and provide for Ruth. Naomi asked Ruth to wash and to put on her best clothes; an act in which I see great symbolism and empowering identity. Ruth had probably worn simple widow's clothes every day up to this point; now for the first time in a long while she was allowed to dress and see herself as a woman again instead of a widow. Taking new courage and strength from this, Ruth followed Naomi's directions. Going late at night to where Boaz was sleeping outside, guarding his grain, she laid down at his feet. I wouldn't think she was able to sleep, but instead I imagine she reflected on her vow to Naomi and prayed to the Lord for even more favour than He had shown her before. About midnight, Boaz stirred, and Ruth had her script ready to be delivered. There was no turning back now. Understandably startled by her presence, Boaz asked who she was. Ruth then quietly but boldly petitioned for Boaz to both marry her, by "taking her under his wing", as well as play out his role as Naomi's kinsman-redeemer. The kinsman-redeemer was responsible for buying land back from his relative's childless widow and providing the widow with an heir; one that would inherit the land and continue the initial family line. It required a sacrifice of money and personal inheritance but was an important aspect of Yahweh's covenant law. Boaz probably took a moment to consider what was going on; there was a lot of information to take in all at once. Quickly, however, he put Ruth at her ease and assured her that she would be provided for; if not by him, then by the kinsman who was closer in line. He would see to the matter. For now, she must not return home alone in the dark, but remain where she was until morning. Now, Ruth really couldn't sleep, though she must have tried hard. The enormous pit in her stomach began to melt into a river of peace. Though this was primarily a business transaction, I'm sure there were deep emotions of mutual affection present as both parties began to envision what they would like to see happen tomorrow. They may have been two people alone in the dark, but I believe that God was there, shining His light into their hearts. A woman's courage and a man's sacrifice, inviting the presence of God – not unlike another Bethlehem night to come when the Saviour of the world would be brought forth in the darkness.

Morning came, and as a gesture of security and promise, Boaz filled Ruth's shawl with as much grain as she could hold. A generous offering indeed! Off Ruth ran in the early morning light to wait impatiently with Naomi for the events of the day to unfold. Naomi must tell Ruth to sit still; no doubt she was second-guessing her boldness and replaying the events of the night over and over again in her mind. As Boaz travelled to the city gate, he devised a plan of his own. He would like to marry Ruth. In spite of being a foreign barren widow he was strongly drawn to her courageous spirit and loyal character. However, we might wonder, why does he feel drawn to actually marry her? He is a rich, honourable Israelite man; she is a poor, barren, foreign widow. Eyebrows would be raised; perhaps his business dealings would suffer. Certainly he already knew and was calculating the financial costs required to fulfill the role of kinsman-redeemer. Yet there is something else about Boaz that is not mentioned here directly, but which could very well be the reason why he didn't see Ruth's circumstances and background as obstacles. You see, *Rahab was Boaz's mother.* You can find it mentioned in Matthew 1:5. Boaz would therefore have been raised in a home that revered and honoured Yahweh and the true spirit of covenant law, and where his mother's testimony of courage and faith would have been told and retold until it was woven and grafted into his spirit as sure as the red cord she probably kept to signify her former life. To Boaz, Ruth's courage and loyalty to Naomi were traits familiar to him, and all that truly mattered; if God could use a former prostitute for His glory, he could use Ruth, and open her womb for His purposes.

At the gate, Boaz didn't have to wait long before the closer relative came by. Asking him to sit down and motioning ten elders to join as witnesses, Boaz began his request. At first, he only mentioned the property belonging to Naomi, which the kinsman was willing to redeem. However, Boaz wasn't finished. He explained that through buying the land, he was also committing to marrying and providing for the widow and raising a son to inherit the land back. Oh dear. Land was one thing, but the extra expense, commitment and hassle to take a foreign wife and raise children for another man was another. When the man declined the whole offer, Boaz then publicly took on a duty that wasn't even his - to redeem Naomi and Ruth. What a love! And a powerful symbol of what our Saviour Jesus would do for us on the cross.

So Boaz married Ruth. I like to imagine the tears of joy that filled her eyes as she gained not only a new husband and protector but the very son of Rahab! Just as our God delights in the praises of His people, so he also delights in bringing us together and providing for us in marvelous and unforeseen ways. Through a pair of barren widows God showcased His exceeding, undeserved love and restored to them a home, a provider, and an heir. The story of Ruth ends with the Lord indeed opening her womb and bringing forth Obed. As the child born out of the kinsman-redeemer transaction, Obed secured both Naomi's and Boaz's family line, and went on to become the grandfather of King David, a direct ancestor of Jesus. Not only does the story of Ruth teach us about the character of the God we serve, but it poignantly identifies us as each having a part to play, even those of us who are barren and ostracized, in the epic story of God's redeeming love.

This week, read the Book of Ruth, putting yourself in Ruth's shoes every step. Journal what God speaks to you through your experience. Do you feel disqualified, or like an outsider in a place in your life right now? Are there others around you who need you to show kindness or act as a redeemer like Boaz? Let the Lord lift your eyes to the fields white with harvest, as he directs your provision and your purpose.

Honour & Shame

I love studying the women of the Old Testament. Though their circumstances, choices, and measure of faith vary, we can learn so much from each one. I even love studying their restrictive and oppressive culture because it makes the actions of these women all the more inspiring. For example, the cultural dynamic of honour and shame weighed heavily upon women in that patriarchal society, closely dictating their behaviour. And yet many of these women rose up in courage, bravery, and faith – even against powerful cultural odds and the stigma of shame – to follow their deeper convictions of righteousness and justice. Four of these women are particularly interesting because of the surprising honour they are later bestowed as named ancestors in the genealogy of Jesus.

In Matthew 1, we find a detailed genealogy of Jesus the Messiah, the son of David, the son of Abraham. Indeed, it is a detailed and orderly chronicle of the male line from Abraham to Jesus, with one small twist. *It also mentions four women.* Women are not usually included in genealogies, so Matthew's readers surely would not have expected a genealogy of Jesus himself to include them. So why are they mentioned? This is something worth investigating, for sure.

I used to think that Matthew mentions these particularly flawed women in order to observe that Jesus didn't have a perfect family and that God can use anyone for His purposes. But the more I study these women and let myself live through their stories, the more I see this genealogy written as a vehicle for bestowing immense honour long overdue. These four women had much in common: they were all foreigners (not born into an Israelite tribe) who came to trust the God of Israel and who asked boldly for a blessing. Unlike other women around them who shrunk back in fear and shame, these women *held deep convictions and acted upon them.* Wow! Now that's a woman after God's own heart! Let's examine each one a little further.

First, there is Tamar. Her name means 'palm tree', and we find her story in Genesis 38. Tamar is a Canaanite taken as a wife for Judah's son Er. Yet when both Er and his brother Onan die for dishonoring God, the widowed Tamar is returned to her father's house. Though Judah has promised to give her to his third son Shelah when he grows up, he doesn't mean to keep his promise, and Tamar knows it. Now a middle-aged childless widow, Tamar could have resigned herself to a quiet life of shame in the shadows, living off the pity and condolences of others. But instead, Tamar determines to take action. She disguises herself as a prostitute and intercepts Judah on the road. He gets her pregnant and leaves his seal with her as a promise of payment. When he is later told that his daughter-in-law is guilty of prostitution, he orders her to be burned to death! Only after she shows him his own seal does he repent, saying, "she is more righteous than I, since I wouldn't give her to my son Shelah" (Genesis 38:26). When Tamar's twins are being born, the babies fight to determine who will arrive first, and the one born first is named 'Perez' (breakthrough). Yes, it's a very strange story, but looking deeper I see a powerful faith at work. I see Tamar sensing the favour that was upon Judah and his family, and a desire to continue his family line. She is determined to see righteousness and justice come to pass through holding Judah to his promise, and I'm incredibly inspired by Tamar's tenacity of spirit exerted against the heavy backdrop of cultural shame to the point of death! Just like a palm tree that grows tall and strong in hot, arid climates, Tamar personifies courage, and is subsequently honoured in Matthew 1 as an ancestress of Jesus Christ.

Next, we meet Rahab, whose name means 'storm' or 'sea monster'. We find her story in Joshua 2 & 6. Of the four women, Rahab has the most reason to feel shame and the most amount to lose. As a Jericho prostitute with a house and family to support, she defies the King of Jericho's orders and hides the Israelite spies. Why? This is what she tells the spies: "I know that the Lord has given you this land and that a great fear of you has fallen on us, so that all who live in this country are melting in fear because of you [...] for the Lord your God is God in heaven above and on the earth below" (Joshua 2:9,11). She had to make a choice: she could melt in fear like everyone else or risk her life for the chance to save it. As a prostitute, she knew she had both the connections and the means to get away with hiding the spies, so what I admire the most about Rahab is her request of them to spare her and her parents and siblings. Rather than allowing the weight of shame to silence her as a foreigner, a woman, and a prostitute, she boldly asks for favour in their eyes, and her appeal is granted. Like a storm, Rahab chooses to dictate her own inner environment rather than allow outside forces to do it for her. In her I see a most noble woman worthy of being honored as an ancestress of Jesus Christ.

Directly following Rahab we find Ruth, which means 'friendship'. There's an entire book of the Bible devoted to her story. Ruth is born a Moabite, a people group despised by Israel. She marries an Israelite man whose family has moved to Moab during a famine in Bethlehem. When her husband, father-in-law and brother-in-law die, her mother-in-law Naomi decides to return home. Ruth must make a choice. Now an impoverished, childless widow deep in grief, Ruth has much reason to sulk back in shame and return to her father's house. But she chooses to take the difficult path forward and accompany Naomi back to her home in Bethlehem. Like Tamar and Rahab before her, I believe she sensed the favour of Yahweh upon her late husband's family, and courageously chose to show friendship to Naomi. She boldly declares, "Your people will be my people and your God my God. May the Lord deal with me, be it ever so severely, if even death separates you and me" (Ruth 1:16,17). Upon arriving in Bethlehem, her courage enables her to glean alone in the fields, ultimately winning recognition and favour with Boaz. And just like Boaz' mother Rahab made a bold request of the spies, so Ruth makes a bold request of Boaz to act as her kinsman-redeemer. Resisting the shame inherent in being a despised Moabite and a barren widow, Ruth acts with dignity, discretion and courage. Boaz acts favourably on her behalf, marrying Ruth and bringing forth Obed, the grandfather of King David. Like her name 'friendship' implies, Ruth's strength lies in her courageous loyalty. She is subsequently honoured as an ancestress of Jesus Christ for her unwavering commitment to an old lady, her people, and her God.

Finally, there is Bathsheba. Bathsheba means 'daughter of oath'. Her story begins in 2 Samuel 11-12 and concludes in 1 Kings 1-2. One lovely spring evening, Bathsheba decides to take a bath on the roof of her home to cleanse herself after her period. She feels quite safe and private, as she believes all the young men and their peering eyes are far away on the battlefield. However, she is mistaken. King David himself, who should have been away fighting with them, is still in the palace and walking on his roof. He sees her, desires her, and sends for her. As the wife of a loyal Hittite in David's army, she is obliged to accept. Upon getting her pregnant but unable to cover up his sin, David has her husband Uriah killed in battle. When David asks for her hand in marriage, again, she has little choice but to accept. Soon after, her child is born, but it lives only a few days. Consumed by grief over the loss of her baby, her first husband, and her former life, Bathsheba's only comfort is in David's arms. She soon conceives again and gives birth to Solomon. Now, Bathsheba must make a choice as she considers how to approach her new reality. Will she succumb to feelings of inadequacy and shame in these unfamiliar palatial grounds, surrounded by David's more legitimate wives all vying for favour and position? Their sons are robust, confident, popular ... how could her son even compare with them? Yet the Lord loves Solomon (2 Samuel 12:24) and I believe Bathsheba knew the Lord's favour was upon him. Much of the book of Proverbs – including Proverbs 31 – was written by Solomon *as inspired utterances his mother taught him*. In praising Solomon's wisdom, we often overlook the fact that it was his mother, Bathsheba, who laid the foundation during childhood for him to receive divine wisdom as king. We know she was beautiful, but she must have been incredibly wise and prudent as well, whole-heartedly taking on her role to raise the next king of Israel.

And yet while Bathsheba worked to cultivate and nurture the heart of a king in her son, King David had still to officially appoint Solomon as his heir. In 1 Kings 1, we find one of David's other sons, Adonijah, appointing himself the next king. When Bathsheba hears this, another crucial choice must be made. Will she shrink back in shame, believing that it's for the best because of the questionable way her marriage began? Or will she enter the king's presence uninvited to remind him of his promise? What if he becomes angry, and sentences her to death? Yet like Tamar, Rahab, and Ruth before her, she pushes shame to the side and acts against the odds to petition for favour. "So Bathsheba went to see the aged king in his room. Bathsheba bowed down, prostrating herself before the king. 'What is it you want?' the king asked. She said to him, 'My lord, you yourself swore to me your servant by the Lord your God, 'Solomon your son shall be king after me, and he will sit on my throne.' But now Adonijah has become king, and you, my lord the king, do not know about it. My lord the king, the eyes of all Israel are on you, to learn from you who will sit on the throne of my lord the king after him.' Then King David took an oath: 'As surely as the Lord lives, who has delivered me out of every trouble, I will surely carry out this very day what I swore to you by the Lord, the God of Israel: Solomon your son shall be king after me, and he will sit on my throne in my place'" (1 Kings 1:15-18,20,29-30). David was a great king, but through Bathsheba's courage and determination his son Solomon both succeeded and superseded him. As a 'daughter of oath', Bathsheba took her vows seriously, making the most of her unplanned circumstances and refusing to allow shame to rob her son of his destiny. As a result, King David swears an oath in her favour, and when King Solomon is crowned he honours his mother, setting her upon a throne at his right hand! A fitting finale for a life nobly lived as an ancestress of Jesus Christ.

There is also a fifth woman mentioned in Matthew 1, which is Mary, the mother of Jesus. Having been visited by an angel proclaiming that she will give birth to God's Son, Mary says, "I am the Lord's servant. May your word to me be fulfilled" (Luke 1:38). Again, here is a woman choosing to take on cultural shame and disgrace, even the possibility of death, to trust God. Her reaction is not one of fear but of praise, thanking God for his merciful justice: "He has brought down rulers from their thrones but has lifted up the humble" (Luke 1:52). Mary's faith is amazingly strong in one so young; but with the Holy Spirit now overshadowing her, she is assured that the cultural shame inherent in her fate will eventually turn to great honour, and she rests in knowing that God is the true judge of her character.

Through the great courage, boldness and faith of these five women, Jesus Christ, our Messiah and Saviour, was brought into our world. But through this same courage, boldness, and faith, *he was led to die on a cross*. To be crucified on a cross was the ultimate shame in Jewish culture. If the Messiah had to die, why couldn't he die as a hero in battle, with full military honours? Many disciples doubted or turned away simply because of his manner of death, believing that "anyone who is hung on a pole is under God's curse" (Deut. 21:23). Yet the author of Hebrews addresses this point, stating that "for the joy set before Him he endured the cross, *scorning its shame*, and sat down at the right hand of the throne of God" (Hebrews 12:2). For those who could see the significance of the shame and ridicule under which Jesus died, most of whom were women, there was incredible comfort given. They could see the greater extent of sin's curse that Jesus was taking on their behalf and embrace a greater joy for the future. Even as soon as Jesus' resurrection, when women were used to proclaim the good news, did women begin to see their way to walk in a purpose equal to that of men. Even today the struggle against shame is still real, but we can scorn shame like Jesus did, enduring our hardships with patience and with our eyes fixed on the joy to come. If

Tamar, Rahab, Ruth and Bathsheba could do it before the cross, you can certainly do it today. Your honour and joy awaits.

This week, read the genealogy of Jesus in Matthew 1, pausing to reflect on each woman's story as she is mentioned. Which woman inspires you the most? Which do you most identify with? Journal your thoughts, noting ways in which you are inspired to persevere or petition for a blessing rather than succumbing to shame. Then bring your heart's cry to Jesus, allowing him to wash you clean from all shame and fill your heart with joy.

Healing Tears

We women are strongly driven by emotions. It's part of how God has made us. Yet in our efforts to control our emotions or force them to conform to some stoic structure, we can do great damage to the souls God gave us. To begin with, have you ever taken the time to think about why and how we cry? When we were babies, we basically cried when we were in need. Whether physical or emotional, it was our means of communication. Once we learned to talk, we could express our daily needs more clearly, but we were still prone to tears at any sudden onset of pain, fear, or loss. Now as adults, we have learned to analyze our feelings, which is good, but also to dismiss and suppress them, which is not so good. The battle for a woman's heart is a messy, emotional business. The devil would love to make you feel alone, undesirable, and inadequate. He will cleverly bring up painful memories from your past, so that the daily demands of the world force you to operate in a robotic, survival mode. Everything is suppressed. You'd rather feel nothing than feel the pain. It's a very real way of life for so many women. Yet what is the one thing that makes human beings different from other species? Our soul. Our mind, will, and emotions. And only God can show us how to keep the three in balance.

We all know that tears are physical. We can feel them, see them, and taste them. Yet have you ever stopped to think how something so physical can be caused by something so abstract as emotion? There is no doubt about it: *Feelings are real.* Never dismiss or suppress your feelings simply because they are an abstract reality or they don't make logical sense. Always remember the spiritual battle raging around you all the time, and that you need to give yourself permission to cry occasionally. Whenever you feel overwhelmed by your emotions, collect your burdens, fears, worries, and hurts and bring them to God, laying them all down at His feet. Next, let the tears flow. Tears bring healing. They are meant to bring refreshment to the desert of your soul. Picture Jesus' taking your burden upon His own strong shoulders, making it appear so much smaller in light of Who now carries it. Then allow His embrace to carry, protect, and nourish *you*, and your weeping and broken soul. I think there is great symbolism in the promise God gives us in the Bible that "[He] will wipe away every tear from [our] eyes" (Rev. 21:4). Its context is meant for heaven, but it's symbolic of how God moves right now. He can't wipe away tears until we allow ourselves to cry.

The reason why crying is so essential is because it can only happen when we are honest, genuine and vulnerable with God. Just like when you would cry unhindered as a child. Becoming child-like is so essential for this journey of restoration. Consider the frightening alternatives: thinking you don't need God, you have Him figured out, or you think you can hide things from Him. By adopting any of these mindsets you are severely grieving His Spirit and diminishing what He desires to do in your life. In other words, just knowing about God is not enough – out head knowledge must also penetrate and change our hearts. Human hearts were created to be softened by the Holy Spirit, in response to His love and power. They were meant to pour out genuine, honest, and vulnerable emotion at Jesus' feet, with tears as our assurance of that essential process at work.

Let's take this one step further now. Just looking at the mystery of the Trinity, we know God is the author of intimate relationship. Crying tears of deep emotion before God is a vital, life-giving experience that can happen as often as every day during times of grief, or as you feel the Lord's presence during worship, prayer, and meditating on Scripture. The Bible says that one day we will stand before God alone and give an account of ourselves. There will be no excuses, nothing to hide behind. Our genuine, honest hearts will finally be revealed. Yet there is something uniquely profound that can happen when you share your brokenness and tears with another person. Having an accountability partner to agree in prayer with and confess your sins to brings honour and glory to God in a manner not possible otherwise. Can you identify with the sinful woman in Luke 7:36-38? She knew she was a sinner, and she chose to confess and mourn her sins to Jesus publicly with tears. Her desperate boldness brought criticism and scorn from onlookers, but she left His presence forgiven and whole. Are you more concerned with how others see you, or how the Lord sees you? Working through this question is an important first step. Next comes asking the Lord to direct you to a mature Christian woman or close friend who can hold you accountable and agree with you in prayer. The unity that is cultivated through genuine emotional vulnerability between believers is incredibly edifying, and expressing tears in this context can bring even greater breakthroughs in your life. Jesus said, "truly I tell you that if two of you on earth agree about anything they ask for, it will be done for them by my Father in heaven. For where two or three gather in my name, there am I with them" (Matthew 18:19-20). The Lord, as the ultimate example of humility, will likewise bless those who demonstrate humility before Him, particularly in the presence of others. So what is the deepest burden of your heart? Big or small, if it matters to you, it matters to God. Don't suppress your emotions or ignore them, but rather let a humble release of tears carry your heart's cry to the feet of Jesus.

This week, reflectively journal about your emotional life with God. If you are self-conscious about crying, go someplace alone and take an honest look at what grieves you the most about the world and your present circumstances and release them to Him, with tears if necessary. Feelings are real and important, and His arms are big enough to carry the full weight of them. As you journal your plans, prayers, feelings, and fears, allow His arms to embrace your heart today.

Your Shield

In this battle we call life, we are in constant need of defense and protection. Throughout the Old Testament, God is praised as being our shield and our defender. Psalm 28:7 declares, "The Lord is my strength and shield. I trust Him with all my heart. He helps me and my heart is filled with joy. I burst out in songs of thanksgiving."

Though we might picture a shield as a small, flat piece of metal carried in the front, God's shielding is praised as surrounding the entire soldier. Psalm 3:3 states, "But you, O Lord, are a shield *around* me, my glory, and the lifter of my head." Psalm 5:12 says, "Surely, Lord, you bless the righteous; you *surround* them with your favour as with a shield." God even declares himself to be a shield to Abraham, telling him in Genesis 15:1 "Fear not, Abram, I am your shield, your very great reward." Clearly the shield of the Lord's presence was something very desirable, and such complete protection unattainable by any physical means. The clearest picture of this is seen in 1 Samuel 17 when David defeats Goliath without using any armour or weapons of warfare because they were too heavy and inhibiting for him to wear. Goliath, on the other hand, approached David fully armed, carrying a spear and led by a shield bearer, but was no match for David's faith in God.

It's interesting to find a few prophetic references in the Psalms to Jesus being our shield. King David's thanksgiving song recorded in both 2nd Samuel 22 and Psalm 18 recounts, "As for God, his way is perfect: The Lord's Word is flawless; he shields all who take refuge in him." The Lord's Word is Jesus, for John 1:14 declares that the Word became flesh and dwelt among us. Psalm 84:9 is even clearer, stating "Look on our shield, O God; look with favour on your *Anointed One*" (which means '*Christ*'). This side of the cross, we believe that Jesus victoriously fought the battle for us, and now through faith in His Name we have this same protection.

In the New Testament, there is only one use of the word 'shield'. The apostle Paul commissions Christians to take on the armour of God: "Take up the shield of faith, with which you can extinguish all the flaming darts of the evil one" (Ephesians 6:16).

Written during the Roman period, the original hearers would have had a clear frame of reference for how this armour worked and looked like. The Roman shield, (Latin 'scutum'), had the shape and size of a large oblong door, with a curved, convex shape. It was designed to give the Roman soldier full body protection when attacked. It was also decorated in elaborate designs that represented specific Roman gods, like Jupiter, or a mighty beast, like a lion. The Latin word 'scutum' has since developed into our modern English word 'escutcheon' (i-SKUCH-en) which refers to an object of *identity* as well as one of protection. It can be defined as a heraldic shield displaying a coat of arms, or the part of a ship's stern where the name is displayed.

If a shield was meant to represent one's *identity* as well as offer protection, then what could your shield say about you? What is your family's spiritual legacy, coat of arms, or regalia, if you will? In other words, what does your faith in Jesus truly symbolize for you? What biblical promises or themes have become such a part of you that they could be inscribed upon your shield? What victories have you experienced that could be a part of your emblem? Are there dents or burns on your shield that tell the world of the darts you have extinguished and the saving grace of God in your life?

I took some time recently to design my own spiritual 'shield' or 'coat of arms'. It's quite an interesting exercise – I encourage you to try it. Mine has a crown at the top, representing my royal status as a daughter of the King of Kings. The shield shape is then surrounded by climbing roses, my favourite flower. Inscribed on the shield, however, is the most important part: my life verse reference (Isaiah 58:11), and my life mission statement (Empathize, Encourage, Educate). I came up with my mission statement through extensive self-reflection and prayer, where I pieced together these three progressive tools that I feel called to bring to a hurting world. In writing this book, for example, I try my best to first empathize with you and your own situation, knowing that it differs from my own. I then try to encourage you along your faith journey, cheering you on, and inspiring you to cultivate a closer walk with Jesus. Only then, after honour is bestowed and relationship established, do I leverage my call to educate using insights gleaned from God's Word.

This is *my* life mission, but we all have a unique faith story, unique giftings, and a unique call. So this week, take some time to reflect on what's specifically shaped your story and the story that your shield of faith tells to the world. Then try your hand at writing your life mission as a way of keeping your efforts in the battle consistent and focused, remembering Who goes before you and shields you along the way. Then journal your plans, prayers, feelings and fears, as a faith declaration that you are more than a conqueror through Him who loves you!

Reaching Versus Touching:
Measuring Impact God's Way

If you're like me, you enjoy finding creative ways to make a difference in the world and in other people's lives, and ultimately God's kingdom. Yet how often do we rely on our own strength and energy to accomplish what we think will make an impact? How is true impact really measured? There are so many great causes out there and so much work to be done. How do we choose? I often used to wish I could get feedback from the people I influence as to how I'm doing, or if my time would be better spent doing something else. This used to concern me, until I started to contemplate the difference between 'reaching' and 'touching' when it comes to the eternal impact of a person's life and ministry. If you think about it, reaching involves striving and doing, and there's nothing wrong with that. The Bible instructs us to "not become weary in doing good, for at the proper time we will reap a harvest if we do not give up." (Galatians 6:9). Jesus was not idle during his three years of ministry here on Earth; he taught, healed, and blessed people from morning until evening, and even sometimes on the Sabbath. Yet consider what it means to *touch*. It doesn't involve planning or doing, just *being*. Being available; being honest; being courageous. Touching is all about surrendering to the will of God and allowing His Light to shine out through the cracks in our lives. It's no coincidence that the apostle Paul compared us to jars of clay in 2nd Corinthians 3:7, "But we have this treasure in jars of clay to show that this all-surpassing power is from God and not from us." As great as Jesus' miracles were, the single greatest thing He did was to allow Himself to be crucified. The *touch* of that single act of surrender had the greatest impact on our fallen world. So just as reaching involves time and energy, touching requires sacrifice. Touching demands a depth of character and complete trust in God and His plan. Do you find yourself wishing your time, energy and finances were as limitless as your dreams? Young women often have so many big dreams of how they can save the world, and then life happens and they find themselves a housewife with a demanding toddler and a sick baby. It's easy to feel discouraged about your impact when you are measuring it based on your reach, so why not focus instead on your touch? Think of it this way: even if you could give something to the whole world, it would never have as much impact as being the whole world to your child. Your sacrificial touch on those closest to you will always produce the greatest eternal rewards. So, keep your focus on Jesus and on allowing the Holy Spirit to transform you into His image. You'll find it's the best way to spend your life!

Trust in the Lord will all your heart and lean not on your own understanding; in all your ways submit to him, and he will make your paths straight. (Proverbs 3:5-6)

This week, reflect on ways you both reach and touch. It's easy to dismiss those tiny moments that no one sees when you gave that encouraging smile, held that child's hand, or gave up that weekend trip to serve your neighbour. We remember more readily the class we prepared and taught, the mission trip we took, or the camp we directed. Both types of influence are important, but those spontaneous moments of sacrificial touch matter the most to God. As you journal your plans, prayers, feelings and fears, remember to just be. He values you and your surrendered heart more than anything you might accomplish for Him.

Plans and Prayers

In your journal, take the time to write out your plans and goals for the coming month of October.

In what ways does the story of Ruth inspire you?

How has shame been holding you back from stepping into the abundant life God has for you?

What concerns are on your heart today that you need to write out as prayer requests to God, in full faith and without shame?

What do you need to confess to Him?

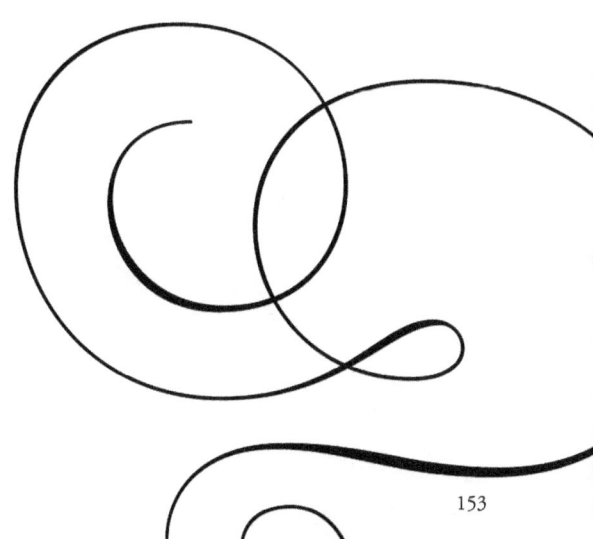

 Feelings and Fears

What are you feeling today?

Do you ever feel frustrated about your limited reach?

Write out how you feel before God, allowing Him to remind you of the power of your touch.

What are you feeling afraid of, or where are you holding the tears back?

Freely journal about whatever comes to mind, as an act of surrendering it all to Him, letting the tears flow.

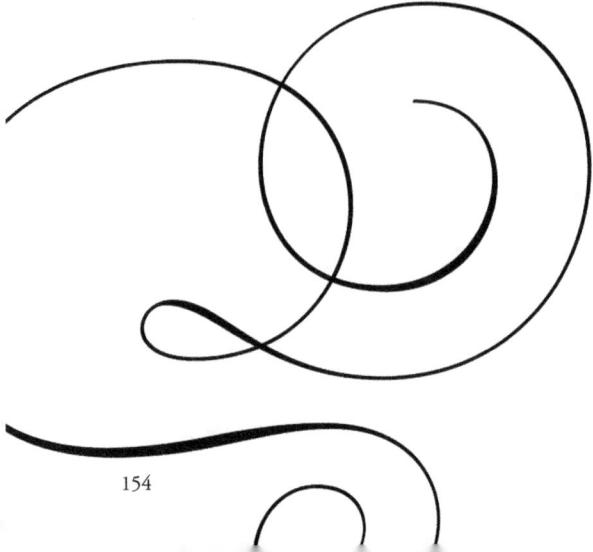

October

The Lighthouse

For centuries, lighthouses served as navigational aids for maritime pilots, like traffic signals on the sea. Lighthouses marked dangerous coastlines, hazardous rocks and reefs, and areas of shallow water. They could also indicate safe entries to harbours. The lighthouse was considered the archetype of public good, indiscriminately offering its light to all in need, free of charge.

In Matthew 5:14-16 Jesus tells us, "You are the light of the world. A city on a hill cannot be hidden. Neither do people light a lamp and put it under a basket. Instead, a lamp is placed on a stand, where it gives light to everyone in the house. In the same way, let your light shine before others, so that they may see your good works and glorify your Father in heaven."

Yet so often when we shine our light before others, they do the exact opposite. This is because "everyone who does evil hates the light and will not come into the light for fear that their deeds will be exposed" (John 3:20). In the absence of light, darkness does have limited power: the power to conceal, to tolerate, and to accommodate. So when light blazes into a dark place, there can be offense, as the power of the dark is taken away and evil exposed for what it truly is. As lighthouses, then, offering light freely to all, we must leave to God how our light is received. Having found safe harbor ourselves, we simply offer it to others, recognizing that many don't understand they are lost in the darkness of the sea and need the help we offer.

As hopeful as a lighthouse is, sea navigators may need more than one exposure in order to find their way to safety. Often it takes many lights to shine on a person over a lifetime. There is such beauty in the way Jesus causes us to work together to bring someone safely to Him, but each one of us is important. Matthew 28:19-20 is our commission: "As you go, make disciples of all nations, baptizing them in the name of the Father and the Son and the Holy Spirit and teaching them to obey all that I have commanded you." Some of us do well at shining compassion in very dark places, while others do well at dispelling shadows of doubt and confusion through instruction. But both are needed to ensure a weary mariner finds his way safely home.

However you feel directed to fulfill your commission, we all need to be prepared and intentional about it. Lighthouses need constant care, mending and maintenance in order to operate properly, and so do we. Matthew 6:22-23 states that "the eye is the lamp of the body. If your vision is clear, your whole body will be full of light. But if your vision is clouded, your body will be full of darkness." So beware of the things you watch, read, and look at. Be intentional at studying God's Word and praying for clear vision. Only then will you be able to see people through God's eyes, and sense how your light should be used to direct them best.

There is an interesting story in the Bible about a prophet named Jonah. God asked Jonah to be a lighthouse to the dark city of Nineveh, but he was first unwilling, then reluctant, and then bitter about the outcome. It is a powerful reminder of the gracious compassion of our God as well as a sobering tale of a lighthouse that had clouded vision. Despite Jonah's imperfections, God saw the Ninevites as people in such spiritual darkness that they couldn't distinguish right from wrong and had compassion on them when they responded to the dimmest of lights shone on them by Jonah.

So, the question remains, how are you managing your lighthouse? Who are you shining on today? How do you regularly refuel your light? Are you even still adrift at sea, oblivious of the danger in the darkness ahead? Always remember the source of light, Jesus Christ, and the power he has to save, heal, and deliver. May you always be a fitting beacon in His service.

This week, reflect on being the light of the world. How does that make you feel? Have you ever offended someone because of your light? Journal some prayers for those in darkness, that they may embrace the light shone on them and not be afraid. How might your lighthouse be clouded? How are you keeping connected to your light source?

SALT & LIGHT

There is a familiar analogy that Jesus uses in Matthew 5:13-16 to describe what His followers should look like: they are to be salt and light. Yet what did that really mean in Jesus' day, and what does that look like for us? To be sure, salt and light in themselves haven't changed over the centuries, but the forms they take have.

First of all, salt in the first century could only be found in various degrees of impurity. The area around the Dead Sea had a particularly high salt content, but it was still important to make the salt as pure as possible in order for it to be effective. Salt lost its saltiness by becoming contaminated. Secondly, light in the first century would have been synonymous with fire. When we read, "You are the light of the world," our first mental image is often a lightbulb, yet there was no electricity in Jesus' day. (A horrible thought, I know!) Jesus' original audience would have pictured the sun's rays or a candle's flame when they thought of light. There is a dynamic and dangerous quality about fire that we lose when we envision the tameness of a lightbulb. The best middle ground would be to think of a bolt of lightning: electricity unharnessed.

Salt and light would also have been staples in first-century households, regardless of family wealth or status. They were available to and needed by everyone, no matter who they were. The same goes for us.

Salt and light complement each other. Salt primarily prevents decay, like a *defense* mechanism against the world. Light dispels darkness, like an *offense* strategy in a sporting event. We need both if we are to win the world for Christ.

Salt and light are also weapons of change for good. Have you ever rubbed salt on a wound, or cooked raw meat over an open flame? Both salt and light have antiseptic properties, burning as they refine and sterilize. If you ever thought being a Christian meant living a tolerant, non-offensive life, think again. Jesus is calling us to stand up against sin, to speak up for the voiceless, and be like salt and flame in the infected wound of the world. Ouch! Will it make people uncomfortable? Yes. Cause hurt feelings? Probably. But if we don't, Jesus says our witness is "no longer good for anything, except to be thrown out and trampled underfoot" (Matthew 5:13). There is of course a right way and a wrong way to approach this. I love this quote by Philip Yancey: "Jesus lived among people with love and humility and brought correction in a way that felt like hope instead of condemnation." Jesus' life demonstrated how it is possible to be pure salt and brilliant light that attracts as it purifies; to offer hope as it kills germs. The difference is love.

As women, God has given us a great capacity to love, and to promote genuine personal relationships in this selfish world. I see a woman's role as salt and light primarily taking an indirect strategy; like entering the enemy's camp through the back door, so to speak. Salt-and-light women can bring their *invasion* of this world through *influencing* and *inspiring* more than *instructing*. There are certainly times when direct instruction is needed, but our witness of 'tough love' is most effective by our subtle proclamation. Instruction speaks to a person's intellect while inspiration speaks to the heart.

When you do feel called to instruct, remember Colossians 4:6, "Let your conversation be always full of grace, seasoned with salt, so that you may know how to answer everyone." What do salty words do? They make things taste better and give people a thirst for more. You don't have to have all the answers. Simply tell others where your faith, hope, and love come from, and how important purity and humility are to maintaining a relationship with the Creator. Salt also melts snow, so believe that the Holy Spirit can use your salty words to melt the hearts of those who need to know Him more.

This week, as you allow Him to fill you with His love, ask Him to use you to influence, inspire, and even instruct. Whether the situation calls you to be a salt-shaker or candle-holder, simply be a vessel willing to be used for His glory.

SCARS

Do you have a scar? Is it a physical burn or cut from a minor accident or injury, or an emotional scar from having grieved the loss of a loved one? We all have scars of some sort, both physical and emotional. What do your scars mean to you? Do they carry painful memories? Do you view them as shameful, secret baggage, or as permission to abuse others and complain about everything? Do you talk about your past wounds openly, hoping for sympathy, or try your best to cover them up? We generally see our scars as ugly and try to hide them. They may even make us feel embarrassed, broken, or damaged. Or perhaps you are someone who is constantly being wounded and are never given the chance to properly heal. Whatever your situation, I encourage you to consider the following points as you reflect on the scars that you carry.

- Scars are reminders of healing. After all, they are no longer wounds, but the remnant of a wound that has been healed. God can't work His powerful redemption in someone who is already perfect, nor can He reveal Himself to someone who is never in need. Once a wound has been healed, the scar remains as a reminder of His healing touch, and therefore of His constant presence with you. So, if you have a wound in your life right now, reach out to God and ask Him to reveal Himself as He leads you on a journey of healing.

- Scars make us each unique. Just as God created each of us differently, your journey of redemption will also be different from everyone else. So instead of your scar making you feel damaged, try thinking of it as making you unique and special. You are one of a kind and designed by God for a specific purpose that only you can fulfill. Your scars and past experiences have put you on a direct path to your destiny, but it's up to you to decide if it's a path of hope or bitterness. Allow God to make it one of hope.

- Jesus had scars. Recall Isaiah 49:15-16a: "Can a woman forget her nursing child, and not have compassion on the son of her womb? Surely they may forget, yet I will not forget you. See, I have inscribed you on the palms of my hands." (NKJV) This prophesy was fulfilled when God sent His Son to earth as a human being, destined to a horrific death on a cross to pay the penalty for our sins. Jesus' perfect body was purposely scarred as a symbol and reminder of how much we mean to Him.

- Scars reassure us that we are becoming more like Jesus. Read II Corinthians 4:10: "[We are] always carrying about in the body the dying of the Lord Jesus, that the life of Jesus also may be manifested in our body." (NKJV) This is a great mystery, but those who live their lives surrendered to the Holy Spirit come to experience its truth. Christians aren't guaranteed a pain-free existence, but we can have peace knowing that when trials come, Jesus is there to say, "Been there, done that. I have the scars to prove it. I'll carry you through."

- Scars keep us humble. The apostle Paul writes in II Corinthians 12 about a physical infirmity of his that the Lord allowed in order that Paul would not become too prideful. As debilitating as it was, and Paul pleaded with God to remove it, Paul instead chose to rejoice in his infirmity. The Lord told him that through it grace would abound, and His strength would be made perfect in weakness. Sometimes wounds can be so severe that we are left permanently disabled. We continue to believe that God can restore wholeness, but we know He sometimes chooses not to in order to perform a deeper work in our heart. It's another great mystery that through our weakness His strength is more perfectly revealed. Through weakness, humility allows us to be able to give Him all the glory, because we know beyond a shadow of a doubt that we can't do it in our own strength.

- Scars cause us to long for heaven. Philippians 3:20-21 says "For our citizenship is in heaven, from which we also eagerly wait for the Savior, the Lord Jesus Christ, who will transform our lowly body that it may be conformed to His glorious body, according to the working by which He is able even to subdue all things to Himself." (NKJV) Scars remind us that this world is not our home! This body and this life that we know today is not all there is; we have great hope of becoming new creations and living forever with Jesus in heaven! Longing for heaven is also a great way to keep daily life in perspective. Whenever I pray, for example, I try to remember to end with 'even so, come Lord Jesus'. More than anything else I desire today, I long to be with my Lord. My scars help keep that desire a daily reality.

- Scars keep us from living complacently. Matthew 11:12 says "The kingdom of Heaven suffers violence, and the violent take it by force." North America has espoused complacency like never before; and all in the name of tolerance and acceptance. We have watered down the Truth to such an extent that it is in danger of disappearing altogether. We need our scars to remind us of the spiritual battle going on, and for us to put on the armour of God every day (see Ephesians 6). When everything is going great, we tend to get lazy and forgetful. May our scars remind us of our duty to fight on behalf of those who are suffering, just as we have known pain in our own lives.

- Scars open doors to sharing our faith with others. Whether your scar is physical and visible or emotional and hidden, it gives you a platform; a place to start a conversation about your journey with someone else in need. Everyone can relate to being weak or infirm at some time, but not everyone has been shown to see their journey of pain as part of God's redemptive plan. They feel shame when instead they should feel hope. Scars can make it easier for you to share with them the hope that you have in Jesus, and to give Him all the glory.

This week, reflect on the scars you have, either physical or emotional. Do they carry shame when instead they should carry hope? Journal your thoughts and feelings about your scars, allowing God to reveal to you the important part they play in His redemptive plan for your life.

Pearls

Aren't pearls stunning? Whether in a solitary setting or strung together as a necklace, pearls have a calming, appealing luster that exemplify class and style. Pearls in nature can be found in a variety of shapes, sizes and even colours. The most expensive ones, of course, are the ones which are perfect – perfectly smooth, perfectly round, and perfectly white. Doesn't that also seem to be how the world measures the value of a woman? Advertising, media, and retail all glorify and cater to 'perfection' in female appearance, leaving all of us in doubt of our value and self-worth because we know it's unattainable. Yet we still try. Why? There is a constant craving in women to look beautiful so they can feel valuable. This lie has even penetrated the church. The good news is that as Christian women, we have all the tools we need to reverse this mindset and redefine what being a woman of value really means. And we need look no further than the pearl.

Have you ever reflected on how a pearl is made? In nature, an oyster has a hard outer shell to protect its tender inner tissue, and for the most part it lives out its days as happy as a clam (no pun intended.) Occasionally, though, this inner tissue can become sliced or wounded, or an unwelcome particle can get caught inside an oyster's shell. This unexpected wound or annoying irritant disrupts everyday life. It is a constant, nagging presence that can cause great wear and tear if ignored. The oyster must exert great energies to secrete a smooth, healing balm to encapsulate the intruder or cover the wound. Over time, a beautiful pearl is created. We all have known seasons of brokenness and pain in our lives which leave us feeling drained, tired, scarred, anything but beautiful. Yet God wants to use each of those times to create a unique and beautiful pearl in your life; something of great meaning and value for you to showcase to others as proof of God's powerful love. So how does God form these pearls, you ask? We all know many people who go through difficult times and come away with only bitterness and regret. How can we as Christian women demonstrate the truth that God really does work all things together for our good? We find the answer simply by examining the characteristics of pearl development.

First of all, pearls are formed in secret. In the wild, they are found in one of the most remote climates on earth: inside one of millions of oysters piled at the bottom of the ocean. This hiddenness of the heart is likewise essential for every woman of God to have. What do you do during times of stress? Turn on the TV and try to escape? Vent your frustrations to those around you? Or do you take time to be alone with the Lord, asking for His peace and to bring your thoughts back in line with His perspective? Though God doesn't cause pain and grief, He often allows it in order to get our attention. He wants our hearts to be hidden with Him; He is the God of intimate relationship. Only through spending quiet time with God can He form the pearl and reveal His beauty in us.

Secondly, pearls are formed in an environment that is very wet and messy. You may say you know all about God, yet when was the last time you allowed the Holy Spirit to move you to tears? As adults, we have learned how to analyze our feelings, which is good, but also to dismiss or suppress them, which is not so good. The worst pain and grief is the kind that pierces the heart; and the battle for your heart is a messy, emotional business. Tears bring healing and refreshment to the dry, ravaged battleground of your soul. I think there is great symbolism in the promise God gives us in the Bible that "[He] will wipe away every tear from [our] eyes" (Rev. 21:4). Its context is meant for heaven, but it's symbolic of how God moves right now. He can't wipe away tears until we allow ourselves to cry; and this can only happen when we are honest, genuine and vulnerable with God. Just like when you would cry unhindered as a child. Becoming child-like with its tears and mess is essential for pearl formation. Human hearts were created to be softened by the Holy Spirit and to pour out genuine emotion at Jesus' feet, and tears can be our assurance of that essential process at work.

The third factor involved in making a pearl is time. Pearls develop over a period of many years. We live in a society of fast food and quick fixes, and we often forget how God's time differs from ours. "But do not forget this one thing, dear friends: With the Lord a day is like a thousand years, and a thousand years are like a day." (2nd Peter 3:8) During difficult times especially, the pain seems to make time stand still and all we want is for God to intervene quickly. Yet we have to allow God's plans to unfold in His time; to let go of what we are doing and learn to just be His. Like a career resume is to a family tree, so the story of what we do is also strikingly different from the story of who we are. It takes time to grow a deep understanding of our unique identity as a child of God. Learning a new job skill make take only a few months, while learning how to exchange gladness for mourning may take a lifetime.

So how do you measure up on God's scale of beauty? Just remember it's the opposite of the world's definition. The world defines value in terms of uniformity and perfection; God defines it in terms of diversity and brokenness. Who the world would deem worthless and throw away, God longs to rescue and restore simply because they are His. But it must start with a surrendered heart. Only then can the pearls begin to form.

This week, think of what is annoying you or has wounded you, but then picture a pearl being formed around it in your heart. Journal how that treasure makes you feel, and then hold it in open hands before God, allowing Him to use it for His glory. How might more pearls begin to form in the place of current bitterness, shame, or regret? Journal your prayers to Him as an act of surrender - and let the pearls begin to form.

OUR UNCHANGING GOD

We live in a throw-away society; people would rather make a change for something new than put work into maintaining what they already have. Advertising, media and technology have brainwashed us into believing that 'off with the old, on with the new' is the happiest, most efficient way to live. It's an especially poisonous philosophy when people apply it to their relationships and their faith. As soon as problems arise, many are quick to question their commitments and turn their backs on God, believing that any change they pursue will doubtless lead to improvement and greater happiness. No wonder then, with so much change going on around us constantly, it can be incredibly difficult to fathom a God who is *unchanging*. Psalm 102:25-27 says "In the beginning you laid the foundations of the earth, and the heavens are the work of your hands. They will perish, but you remain; they will all wear out like a garment. Like clothing you will change them and they will be discarded. But you remain the same, and your years will never end." Wow... how do we love, and inspire others to love, such an eternal Being as that? With so many new ideas coming at us all the time, and knowing that people embrace them believing they have as much validity as the values that society has held for centuries, how do we as Christians sort through it all in order to demonstrate a timeless message in a timely way? Here's a few thoughts I had:

- Remember that God sees the beginning, the middle and the end. He knows each of us inside out and can see the best path for us to take. People are often reluctant to give up control until they come to a place that is beyond their control. Psalm 33:11 says, "The plans of the Lord stand firm forever, the purposes of his heart through all generations." There is great comfort in reflecting on the fact that God was there at your birth, already knows tomorrow and therefore asks for you to trust Him today.

- Understand the difference between change and improvement. Improvement always involves change, but change isn't always improvement. Adam and Eve first sinned because they desired knowledge more than obedience to God, and that thirst for societal 'improvement' apart from God continues to this day. A perfect, unchanging God has given us rules to govern our lives by, and we must choose to maintain that moral compass in order to properly discern what 'improvement' truly looks like. The story of the prodigal son can be found in Luke 15:11-24. The younger son didn't know how good he had it until he lost it all; he didn't realize that 'change' could be bad. God often allows us to rebel and go our own way in order to help us see the value of the life we had with Him. He then patiently waits for us to return.

- Put a higher value on preventative maintenance. Something of enduring value, whether it is a relationship, the environment, or your health, needs to be cared for or else it will disintegrate. It can't be treated like an iPad; you can't upgrade when your old one burns out. God has given us the task of stewardship - but how much time are we investing in the cultivation of what's most important? May God give us the wisdom we need to fulfill this high calling in spite of what society says. After all, buying into the throw-away mindset only means that in the end, you'll have nothing left to throw away.

"Jesus Christ is the same yesterday, today, and forever." (Hebrews 13:8)

This week, meditate on this verse. How does it initially make you feel? Jesus being the same every day is worlds away from the boredom we connect with breakfast being the same every day. He is more like the air we breathe – we would never want it to change, and we would die if it ever went away. Journal on that concept of an unchanging God, reflecting on the value of dependability and faithfulness that you see in things and people around you. What maintenance measures do you need to attend to in order to preserve your most valued relationships?

Plans and Prayers

In your journal, take the time to write out your plans and goals for the coming month of November.

What scars do you carry?

Have you ever thought of them as pearl potential, or as a platform for your witness as salt and light in God's kingdom?

Journal about the ways you've seen the Lord use your brokenness to help others.

What concerns are on your heart today that you need to write out in faith as prayer requests to God?

What can you thank him for in this season of harvest?

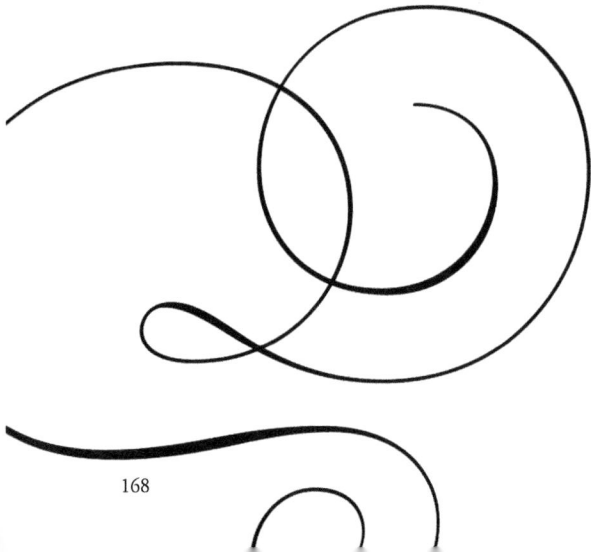

Feelings and Fears

What are you feeling today?

What puzzles you the most about God's nature?

Write out how you feel, affirming your trust in the sovereignty of his mysterious ways.

What are you asking God to change about your life?

Freely journal about whatever comes to mind, as an act of surrendering it all to His higher purposes.

November

The Jeweled Garment

A hundred years ago, there lived a king and queen in a distant and remote country. The land was vast, and so was the king's wealth. The king and queen, who were very happy together, had four beautiful daughters and one son. All was not happy in the land, however. It was a desolate and cold country, and most of the king's people had very little to live on. Soon, the people began to turn against the king and his family and demand that they rule the country themselves. They sent the king and his family away to an isolated part of the country while they raised up their own leader and plotted to kill the king. Shortly after, the king, queen, the four princesses and the young prince were killed by their guards and buried in an unmarked grave.

It is a horrific story, and not a fairy tale. Czar Nicholas II of Russia and his young family were assassinated in July of 1918 by order of the Bolshevic government that deposed them. This is a fact of history. But there are more details to this story and many legends that surround it, and I'd like to ponder a few of them here.

The Czar's four daughters were called the Grand Duchesses Olga, Tatiana, Maria and Anastasia. Though the Czar and Czarina longed for and needed a son, their four daughters were welcomed, loved and cherished before and after their brother Alexei came along. The girls had a happy and close childhood, sheltered from an outside world that was becoming increasingly hostile and embittered towards their father's regime. The sisters would converse happily with anyone they were permitted to meet with, regardless of status, including the very guards who would later carry out orders to execute them. And yet, all their lives, especially during those dark days under house arrest, the princesses knew their lives were in danger. Yet they had their faith, each other, and their closest personal possessions – their jewels – to remind them of who they were.

Jewels have significant symbolism. They are items of great value, rarity, and strength, used to reflect the status of their owners. Normally, the key to this status is their display: in crowns, necklaces, rings, sceptres, or any form of outward adornment. Yet never have jewels served royalty more shrewdly than those belonging to our Russian princesses. During the long days and nights of captivity and isolation, the four princesses took great care to *sew their jewels into the linings of their corsets*. Now, hidden away from view but continually felt, the princesses continued to show kindness to their guards and to each other, still unsure of their destiny but ever mindful of their identity.

I love that part of the story. To me, life as a Christian woman should be like that. Aware of the danger and unsure of the future, she continues to share Christ's love with the world because she is assured of her royal identity and the treasures she has hidden in her heart.

Though the jewels were doubtless sewn into the corsets to prevent them from being lost or stolen, it is very interesting to note that because of the jewels being where they were, the jewels deflected the initial bullets shot at the princesses on that horrific night of execution. Only after multiple rounds and the force of bayonets were the girls finally deemed deceased.

So allow me to pause and ponder for a moment. Brilliant jewels and gemstones that were seemingly hidden away to protect them from theft actually protected their owners instead. Jewels that under normal circumstances had greater value when displayed rather than kept hidden, actually protected and supported human life in a more substantial way as a *foundation garment* rather than an *outward accessory*.

What meaning might you take away from this story? What are the jewels and treasures that give you a sense of self-worth? Would they serve equally well as foundation garments - known only to yourself and God - or does their value depend on being noticed by others? I Peter 3:3-4 tells us that our beauty should not come from outward adornment in hairstyle, clothing, or jewelry, but from the *inner disposition of the heart*, the unfading beauty of a gentle and quiet spirit, which is so precious to God. Do your treasures have the supernatural strength to deflect the bullets of the Enemy? Only by knowing the Word of God and the Holy Spirit's voice can those beautiful jewels also serve as a bullet-proof vest, the strongest of which are pure and refined by fire.

And finally, there is the legend. The legend that one of the princesses miraculously escaped the assassination and was successfully rescued from Russia by one of the guards. The legend has always suggested it to be Anastasia, the youngest of the girls whose name means 'resurrection'. However, they say that Maria was the most personable, affectionate and charming of the four girls, doubtless winning her way into the heart of an unsuspecting guardsman, and Maria's body was indeed missing when they discovered the burial site. Though her rescue and survival are farfetched and merely speculation, I like to view this tragedy as containing an element of hope and the role for a savior to play.

For just as the jewels of our godly character can defer the Enemy but never destroy him, so we are like Maria. We need to remember our need for a Saviour to rescue us from something we could not escape from on our own. Jesus didn't just come to teach us how to live a holy life, but to save us from sin and death. Nothing we could ever do on our own could save us from eternal defeat, only Jesus himself. But when we receive his gift of salvation and trust his guiding hand, he promises to give us not only a jeweled garment, but a jeweled castle! Isaiah 54:11-14 says, "Afflicted city, lashed by storms and not comforted, I will rebuild you with stones of turquoise, your foundations with lapis lazuli. I will make your battlements of rubies, your gates of sparkling jewels, and all your walls of precious stones. All your children will be taught by the Lord, and great will be their peace. In righteousness you will be established: Tyranny will be far from you; you will have nothing to fear. Terror will be far removed; it will not come near you."

What a beautiful promise! Though our jewels are currently hidden, they will one day be revealed and traded up for his jewels and our royal identity as his daughters will be celebrated openly. Revelation 21 describes that day in greater measure: "And he carried me away in the Spirit to a mountain great and high, and showed me the Holy City, Jerusalem, coming down out of heaven from God. It shone with the glory of God, and its brilliance was like that of a very precious jewel, like a jasper, clear as crystal. The wall was made of jasper, and the city of pure gold, as pure as glass. The foundations of the city walls were decorated with every kind of precious stone. The first foundation was jasper, the second sapphire, the third agate, the fourth emerald, the fifth onyx, the sixth ruby, the seventh chrysolite, the eighth beryl, the ninth topaz, the tenth turquoise, the eleventh jacinth, and the twelfth amethyst. The twelve gates were twelve pearls, each gate made of a single pearl. The great street of the city was of gold, as pure as transparent glass."

Yes, life is a struggle. Our world is under attack, and there is suffering and tragedy everywhere. The murder of these beautiful young princesses a century ago could be used as a metaphor for the tragedy and injustice that surrounds us today. But through Christ Jesus our Saviour, we have hope. Romans 8:17 promises us that if we suffer with Him, we may be also glorified with Him. Our present sufferings are not worth comparing with the glory that is to be revealed to us.

So take heart, treasured woman of God! Know his voice. Read his Word. Seek His power. Keep those jewels strategically hidden within your gentle gracious spirit, for "nothing is concealed that will not be uncovered, nor hidden that will not be made known" (Matt. 10:26). Your castle of glory awaits!

This week, think about your possessions that have the greatest value. What items would you grab first if your house were on fire? What things do you keep well-insured, or under lock-and-key? It's fine to invest in valuable things, provided they aren't all that matters. Weigh now those items against intangible things like restful sleep, life-giving friendships, your career, and your children's dreams for the future. Journal freely about how you would respond if these came under attack or were threatened. Then ask yourself, are there things you treasure even deeper still that nothing in this world can threaten to take away? Allow God to reveal these jewels as symbols of your royal identity and inheritance, and then hold them close to your heart like your life depends on them, because it does.

FORGIVEN? FORGIVE

Forgiveness is one of those things that defies human logic. The profound impact that law and justice, right and wrong, and crime and punishment have on the way we think about ourselves and operate in our world often causes us to view forgiveness as an unnecessary appendage to ordered society. What kind of world would this be if we let violent criminals and destructive, evil people have their way unchecked? What about the rights of those they have victimized? The truth is that we are all victims of some kind; no one can live through the vulnerability of childhood and a fledgling adolescence without enduring wounds and regret. At the same token, no one can escape these same years without bringing hurt to others along the way. All humans are prone to sin and have suffered hurt. So in that light, what kind of world would there be without forgiveness? As the saying goes, hurt people hurt people. Only forgiveness can break the cycle.

When God gave Israel His laws in the Old Testament, there was one particular clause, the Year of Jubilee, that He gave as a legal standard for forgiveness. Every fifty years, all slaves were to be given freedom, all unfortified property returned to its ancestral owners, and all the people were to enjoy a harvest provided by the Lord that they didn't plant. This meant that if you had previously declared bankruptcy and had sold your land and then yourself as a slave in order to pay your debts, your debt would be forgiven and you would be free to return to your home in the Year of Jubilee. That's the radical forgiveness of God. Romans 8:20-21 elaborates this theme: "For the creation was subjected to frustration, not by its own choice, but by the will of the one who subjected it, in hope that the creation itself will be liberated from its bondage to decay and brought into the freedom and glory of the children of God." God Himself gave us laws in order that we may see in them how our sin separates us from Him, yet He longs to lavish on His creation a forgiveness that restores our relationship to its former state. Once we recognize our sin, repent from it and embrace the forgiveness He offers, He then commands us to forgive others. Are you forgiven? Forgive.

When we forgive, we still recognize that the sin against us mattered, and that it was wrong. We may need to grieve that loss or hurt, and there may still be punishment required for the offender. But we choose to remove it from the debts we feel are due us. The Greek word used implies letting go; sending away. Jesus tells Peter a parable in Matthew 18:21-35 about a servant who was forgiven a great debt by a king, but in turn refused to forgive a small debt owed him by a lesser servant. The comparison is striking, and yet we are each guilty of harbouring resentment and unforgiveness against others after we've been released from the death penalty ourselves. May we each be like the woman in Luke 7:36-50, whose story paints a beautiful portrait of the love a woman can show when she knows she is forgiven: "Therefore I tell you, her sins, which are many, are forgiven – for she loved much; but he who is forgiven little, loves little" (Luke 7:47, ESV). May we lavish love on our Savior in the same way, letting it spill over into our dealings with all those around us.

As radical and gracious as God's forgiveness is, more astounding still is His ability to forget. Can God really forget? He tells us in Jeremiah 31:34b, "For I will forgive [your] wickedness and will remember [your] sins no more." Now that's a mystery for sure! Yet there are different ways to forget, and I'd like to share an analogy about this that I think will help clarify the confusion. We've all heard that elephants have excellent memories, which is true. They are considered to be one of the smartest mammals on earth. Yet sometimes memory can be a detriment. Once, a baby elephant at the zoo was continually wandering around and getting into trouble, so the zookeeper tied a small chain around her front leg and attached it to a wooden spike in the ground. She would pull on the chain to get free, but with no luck. As the years passed, she stopped pulling on the chain entirely, since her memory told her that all effort was futile. What she didn't realize was that she had grown much bigger during those passing years, and if she were to try to free herself again, she could. What a sad story. We all have painful memories, yet we don't have to allow them to hold us back from our freedom. That's what forgiving and forgetting is all about. Those scars you carry from past wounds, even if they were self-inflicted, have made you stronger, yet your memories of those times have great power to hold you back. Choose to release them, forgiving yourself if necessary, and break those flimsy chains that Jesus has given you freedom from. It's been said that forgiveness involves releasing a prisoner, and then realizing that prisoner was you. So break the cycle of hurt. Forgiven? Forgive.

This week, journal your thoughts about forgiveness, both of yourself and others. Are you having difficulty forgiving someone? Reflect on how you feel about all God has forgiven you from, and then direct that grace to another. Perhaps you have forgiven yourself or someone else, but the painful memories have you bound up in bitterness or regret. Ask God to help you to forget, in the sense that those past events no longer have power over your emotions today. Journal a letter to God, yourself or someone else, as a physical demonstration of your releasing the situation, and then destroy it. Then step into the freedom and joy you were always meant to have.

The Sword of Prayer

Imagine a beautiful maiden extending a sword in the gesture of knighting a young man who kneels before her. He goes down a man and arises a knight. What interchange has just taken place? Why does this man kneel before her?

The woman has transferred something intangible to the young man bowed before her. He kneels because she embodies the very reason and hope for his pledge. He vows to protect all she represents with the edge of his sword and the strength of his might. If war, peril, or great need were to arise, he would count his life forfeit if it meant protecting hers. He has pledged his honor and virtue. I love this image. It conveys the power of feminine virtue and beauty to stir a man to a higher purpose. It is the gentle awakening the strong by bestowing glory.

He does not fear the sword when it is in her hand. In her possession, it is no longer a weapon but an instrument of transformation. It is not presented to threaten, wound, or strike the man; it is extended to set him apart. He is no longer the same. As a knight, his life has been expanded and his name enlarged to encompass a title and eventually a legacy. He has been dubbed and elevated. This means both weight and honor have been added to his name. With the sword, she transfers power and confers something only she can give: a higher purpose and reason to live.

He does not experience the edge of the sword when it is in her hands. He feels the sword's full weight as the flat of it is transferred from shoulder to shoulder. With this solemn act, she grants him the necessary authority and entitlement. He now shoulders the responsibility and honor of the one who bears the sword.[1]

I have a copy of the painting, "The Accolade" by Edmund Blair Leighton hanging in my room. It is an inspiring image, with deep spiritual significance, which I think Lisa Bevere must have had in mind as she describes with expert flair the knighting of a young warrior by his queen. Yet I would like to explore deeper the spiritual significance of how a woman can bestow honour upon her man through the power of prayer.

Prayer is a mighty tool – very much like a sword – that we women seldom use as often or as fervently as we should. Yet a woman's prayers for her husband (or future husband) have an enormous impact on him, and have the power to break strongholds and promote change in his life and in your relationship. Notice the lack of dialogue between the knight and his queen. Her actions and his posture convey the entire message. This doesn't mean you shouldn't communicate with your spouse, but that you should listen to him and pray for him much more often than you should speak. This doesn't rob you of your status, for you know you are a queen, standing tall, with a sword in your hand. Nor does this prevent you from expressing your opinions and feelings verbally, but prayer should be your primary outlet. Proverbs 29:11 is a great verse to meditate on and take to heart: "A fool vents all [her] feelings, but a wise [woman] holds them back." Don't keep your emotional words bottled up or suppressed, but rather release them in a different direction. The Psalms are full of verses that contain raw emotion expressed passionately before God alone – so use David as your guide for becoming the principal prayer warrior for your husband. After all, David was called a man after God's own heart (1 Samuel 13:14), and I hope to become a female version.

---

[1] *Fight Like a Girl: The Power of Being a Woman* by Lisa Bevere. Copyright 2006 by Lisa Bevere. Used by permission of Faith Words/Hachette Book Group USA Inc., pp. 99-100.

What I find particularly beautiful about this image of the accolade is that the woman is using the sword to intentionally bestow honour and glory upon the man. As women, we often desire to control, manipulate, or change our men where instead we should be respecting, trusting, and honouring them. Always remember the sword in your hand, and the power it has to either build up or destroy. Feeling frustrated or angry with your husband? Bring it to the Lord, recognizing and waging war against the spiritual forces that are trying to bring division between you. Do you want to see a change in a certain area of his life? Analyze your motives, and then begin to pray into it fervently. Change will come in time, though recognize that it may come to *you* instead of him. Remember, marriage was God's pinnacle act of creation; His special treasure and delight. He wants to bless and prosper your union even more than you want Him to, but you must allow Him entrance.

Perhaps you are single and praying for a husband. The sword of prayer applies equally well to your situation. God in His mercy knows your longing and your heart, and how you are choosing to wait on His timing. Yet perhaps God wants to use this time to train you to become a better prayer warrior, for you will certainly need to pray just as much after you marry as you do before. Start by visualizing your future husband alone in the world, or perhaps in a bad relationship. What aspects of his life could you be bathing in prayer right now before God brings you together? Certainly protection against temptation and sin, his thought life, his family, his friends, his job, his health, and any other specific aspects the Lord may prompt you to be in prayer for. Many single women make detailed lists of the qualities they are looking for in a husband, and that's not wrong, but perhaps you could make a detailed prayer list instead. Praying for the Lord to prepare Him to be a godly husband and prepare you to be a godly wife is the best possible use you can make of this time the Lord has given you before marriage. Simply remember who you are and what is in your hand.

This week, reflect on your regular prayer habits and posture. Do you usually pray from a position of weakness and petition, or from a place of strength and declaration? God loves to answer your prayer of need, but He longs for you to also pray bigger prayers for the people and the world around you from a position of authority. When it comes to your husband (or future husband), recognizing the enemy's schemes to thwart your relationship and praying against them is of supreme importance. Take time to write out some prayers for each aspect of your man's life and tangible ways you can show him honour and respect, as a royal princess would knight her prince.

A Beautiful Exchange

The Gospel is all about transaction. Be it an instantaneous miracle or a gradual process, our God delights in offering us renewal and new birth in exchange for our old selves. The prophet Isaiah spoke about this coming divine substitution in Isaiah 61:1-3:

> *The Spirit of the Sovereign Lord is on me, because the Lord has anointed me to proclaim good news to the poor. He has sent me to bind up the brokenhearted, to proclaim freedom for the captives and release from darkness for the prisoners, to proclaim the year of the Lord's favor and the day of vengeance of our God, to comfort all who mourn, and provide for those who grieve in Zion – to bestow on them a crown of beauty instead of ashes, the oil of joy instead of mourning, and a garment of praise instead of a spirit of despair. They will be called oaks of righteousness, a planting of the Lord for the display of his splendor.*

What a beautiful exchange! In our finite minds, though, such a reality seems like it belongs in a fairy tale rather than as a true possibility. There is a law of physics called entropy, which states that all matter is constantly progressing towards disorder. Metal will rust; people will get old and die. Whether or not we've ever studied physics, we all seem to be very much aware of the downward spiral of life. We therefore need constant reminding of God's goodness, and how this same God is the Creator of the laws of physics and is using them as tools in His greater story of Redemption. So let's revisit these three dramatic exchanges that Isaiah foretold: beauty for ashes, joy for mourning, and praise for despair.

- Beauty for Ashes: As women, our sense of self-worth is closely linked to our perception of our own beauty. How such a fleeting and abstract sentiment as beauty can have such a firm grip on us emotionally puzzles us constantly; yet we are each keenly aware of the detrimental effects of feeling ugly, unkempt, or unloved. Our attitudes, language, posture, diet, everything begins to fail when we allow those bitter ashes to pile up. Try as we might to reverse the damage, we need to recognize how our desire to showcase beauty reveals our need for a Saviour. Only Jesus can exchange the ashes in our hearts for unimaginable beauty; only He can transform us from feeling *ravaged to ravishing*.

- Joy for Mourning: There is no greater pain in life than the loss of a loved one. Whether or not we had the assurance of their salvation, the pain of grief can become overwhelming. Nothing seems to bring comfort; even reliving happy memories or cherishing the people who remain can seem to push the sword deeper into our heart. We all know life as a battle, so when someone we love dies, it's natural to feel a sense of defeat. Our faith can easily become shaken as we wrestle with feelings of loss, regret, and failure. The only way out is to turn to Jesus. His joy is the perfect antidote to your grief; His hope the only answer to your defeat. Only Jesus can exchange our desert of mourning for the oil of joy; turning the *most beaten into the brightest beacon*.

- Praise for Despair: Even when life seems to be going along okay, there are still many of us who see the glass as half-empty rather than half-full. Fear of the unknown can grip even the most optimistic of us, and insurance companies stay in business because of our fear of losing what we have. Uncertainty is part of life; it is another shadowy sentiment meant to remind us of our need for the Lord and our mission to help others, yet how often do we use it as an unspoken excuse to become self-absorbed? This heaviness often goes unnoticed as we go about our busy lives, working to try and maintain an impossible standard. Only until we take the time to look to Jesus do we realize how much of a burden we are needlessly carrying. Only Jesus can turn our wooden yoke of heaviness into a luxurious garment of praise. Only with His praise in our hearts can we fight for His purposes instead of our own; a *worrier can become a warrior.*

What's the purpose of this beautiful exchange? What's the motivation behind this unmerited favour? The answer is clear: so that we might be like oak trees of righteousness planted by the Lord, bringing Him glory. We are His workmanship, and the sheep of His pasture. He longs to bestow on us His beauty, joy, and praise in exchange for our ashes, mourning, and despair. The ravaged can become ravishing, the beaten a beacon, and the worrier a warrior. And it's all because of Jesus.

This week, reflect on how the gospel is about exchange; how your old burdens, mindsets and identities were traded up for heavenly ones when you accepted Christ. Write out some truths from God's Word that you can post on your mirror or fridge as a reminder, such as: I have the mind of Christ. I am clothed in strength and dignity. I am seated in heavenly places. As you close your prayers each day, visualize Jesus physically lifting your burdens off your shoulders and giving you something sweet to eat. He is the Master of the Beautiful Exchange.

Your Crowns in Christ

Since ancient days, crowns have been used to bestow honour and symbolize rank. Yet in the Old Testament, kings of Israel were anointed rather than crowned. The first mention of a royal crown, *kathar*, given to an Israelite is in the book of Esther. "Now [King Xerxes of Persia] loved Esther more than all the other women. He was so delighted with her that he set the royal crown on her head and made her queen instead of Vashti" (Esther 2:17). She not only was given honour but was appointed to a new royal rank.

Yet the more common word used in the Old Testament to convey the idea of a crown is *atarah*. It is used figuratively to suggest honour, given to those whose conduct is pleasing to the Lord. Wearing a crown like this requires poise, strength, and an upright posture. It bestows so much more than honour; it causes a change in perspective. With the head lifted in support of the glory it bears, the eyes point upward and outward to their Source of strength and to a world in need. Proverbs 4:9, for example, promises a graceful garland for the head, like a beautiful crown, for those who cherish and walk in wisdom. And Proverbs 12:4 observes that a wife with strength of character is the crown of her husband. A wife plays a crucial role in her husband's success, offering him glory and honour through her godly conduct.

By the Greek period in history, a crown (*stephanos*) in the form of a wreath or garland was regularly awarded to victors in athletic competitions. This word is then used several times in the New Testament to communicate a desirable award or medal of merit.

The use of *stephanos* is made even more poignant, therefore, when it is used to describe the 'crown of thorns' Jesus is made to wear during his crucifixion. Not only is honour made to inflict shame, but glory becomes physical pain as the sharp thorns pierce his brow. It is also interesting to observe that thorns themselves did not come into existence until after Adam's sin (Genesis 3:18), powerfully signifying the weight of creation's curse that Jesus took upon Himself. They were never part of the original created order, yet Jesus bore both their curse and their pain so that we could be crowned with Him for having endured the same curse in His name.

And yet, the crown of thorns is still a crown, and Jesus still a King. Because Jesus was obedient to the Father even to the point of death on a cross, God honoured his name above all other names and promises certain crowns to those of us who will do the same. The other instances of *stephanos* mentioned in the New Testament refer to heavenly crowns promised to faithful Christians based on their earthly conduct.

The Crown of Righteousness is mentioned in 2 Timothy 4:8. Paul, at the end of his life, rejoices because of the hope of this crown. "Now there is in store for me the crown of righteousness, which the Lord, the righteous Judge, will award to me on the day of his return. And not only to me, but to all who eagerly look forward to his appearing." When you have heaven constantly on your mind, longing for the end of pain and death and to see you Saviour face-to-face, you won't be able to help living a righteous life. The only thing that matters to you is pleasing Him and walking worthy of the calling and identity He has given you.

The Imperishable Crown mentioned in 1 Corinthians 9:24-25 has the closest meaning to the cultural Greek. Paul observes, "Don't you realize that in a race everyone runs, but only one person gets the prize? Run so that you may obtain it! Everyone who competes in the games trains with strict discipline. They do it for a crown that is perishable, but we do it for a crown that is imperishable." The Imperishable Crown, therefore, will be awarded for endurance and discipline. Races were not sprints, but marathons. Discipline was necessary to train before the race, and endurance necessary to reach the finish line. So keep that in mind as you keep your eye on the prize.

The Crown of Life is reserved for those who persevere under great trial. James 1:12 says, "God blesses those who patiently endure testing and temptation. Afterward they will receive the Crown of Life that God has promised to those who love Him." Revelation 2:10 adds, "If you remain faithful even when facing death, I will give you the Crown of Life." Courage and fortitude is necessary at all times, but especially when experiencing persecution. The Church has experienced great persecution and martyrdom over the centuries, and Jesus promises those who endure severe testing a special honour.

The Crown of Glory is promised to those who teach and shepherd Christians well. 1 Peter 5:2-4 states, "Care for the flock that God has entrusted to you. Watch over it willingly, not grudgingly; not for what you will get out of it, but because you are eager to serve God. Don't lord it over the people assigned to your care but lead them by your own good example. And when the Great Shepherd appears, you will receive the Crown of Glory that will never fade away." James 3:1 then adds, "Not many of you should become teachers, because you know that we who teach will be judged more strictly." Leading and teaching other believers requires a special maturity of character, and a lifestyle of greater holiness. But the reward is great for such as these, namely the Crown of Glory.

The Crown of Exaltation is the most unique of all, for it is a crown made of people. For those who dedicate their lives to bringing others into a saving knowledge of Jesus, the joy of seeing these new converts in heaven will be their reward. Paul says in Philippians 4:1, "brothers and sisters, stay true to the Lord. I love you and long to see you, dear friends, for you are my joy and my crown." He adds in 1 Thessalonians 2:19, "who is our hope, or joy, or crown of boasting, before our Lord Jesus at His coming? Is it not you?" Their reward will be the most visible honour of all the crowns in heaven, for nothing is more precious to God than people who have accepted His saving grace and chosen to walk in obedience to Him.

We can be assured that heaven will be more glorious than we could even dare imagine, and I want to be adorned in some of that glory by my Lord, no matter what the cost. Isaiah 62:2-3 prophesies of this glorious hope to come: "The nations will see your vindication, and all kings your glory; you will be called by a new name that the mouth of the Lord will bestow. You will be a crown of splendor in the Lord's hand, a royal diadem in the hand of your God." God bless you as you hold onto that hope today.

Margaret Frost once said, "People are encouraged to become their best when you hold a crown just a little above their heads and ask them to grow into it." Journal your thoughts about this statement, and how you feel about doing things to obtain a reward. Hebrews 12:2 says that Jesus endured the cross because of the joy set before Him. Begin to imagine what it will be like to stand before Jesus in Heaven as he puts a priceless golden crown on your head saying, 'well done, good and faithful servant'. How will that make you feel? How does that encourage you to serve Him with greater faithfulness and endurance today?

Plans and Prayers

In your journal, take the time to write out your plans and goals for the busy month of December.

In what ways can you make Advent a particularly meaningful season this year?

How has reflecting on all Jesus has done for you through the Beautiful Exchange deepened your anticipation for Christmas and for His second coming?

This can be a particularly depressing, stressful, and lonely time of year for many people. What individuals are on your heart to pray for? Record them in your journal, to both pray for them and connect with them during the coming month.

What do you looking forward to the most in this next season?

FEELINGS AND FEARS

What are you feeling today?

What do you tend to do when your feelings get hurt?

Write out how you feel before God, remembering that He desires to cultivate all of these things as jewels in the secret place.

What are you worried about today?

Freely journal about whatever comes to mind, as an act of surrendering it all to Him.

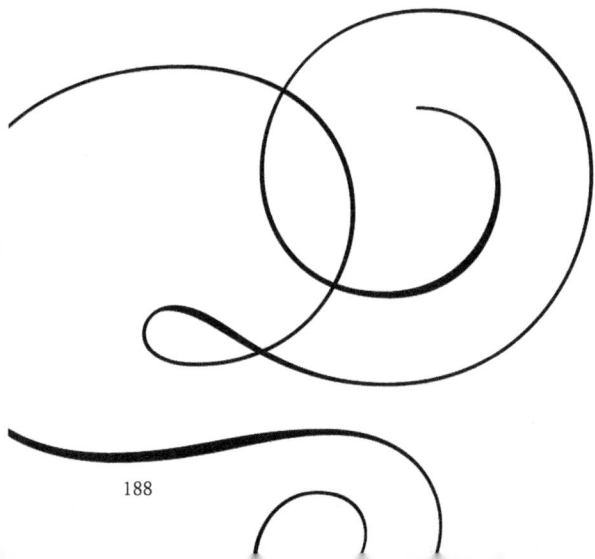

December

IF SHAKESPEARE WAS JESUS

Romeo & Juliet is one of the most famous love stories in literature, despite its tragic ending. The themes of hatred, conflict and forbidden love resound in our hearts because they are easily recognized in both our society and in ourselves. Even the tragic death of the principal characters at the end only increases our affinity for the story, as we are reminded of our own losses. The Bible tells an epic story, too; one of great conflict and tragedy, fear and defeat, love and loss. Yet this grand story differs from Shakespeare's in several ways: it is true, it has a happy ending, and its author is also the main character. Isaiah 53:3-5 describes the coming Messiah: "He was despised and rejected by mankind, a man of suffering, and familiar with pain. Like one from whom people hide their faces he was despised, and we held him in low esteem." This coming Messiah would be Jesus, the Author of the story, and would come with a mission, as Isaiah continues: "Surely He took up our pain and bore our suffering, yet we considered Him punished by God, stricken by Him, and afflicted. But He was pierced for our transgressions, he was crushed for our iniquities; the punishment that brought us peace was upon Him, and by His wounds we are healed."

God is both the Author and the Hero in His Redemption story. The climax of all human history was Jesus' death on the cross. There, humanity and eternity intersected; the ultimate sacrifice was provided by God himself in order to reconcile us back to Him and to each other. Can you imagine if Shakespeare himself were to appear as the hero in the last act of *Romeo & Juliet* and save the pair from committing suicide? Wouldn't that have changed things! How much more reason would the Montagues and Capulets have had to reconcile their differences!

Yet *would they*? Would they have recognized Shakespeare as their author and creator, first of all, and how only he could bring about an end to their feud? Would they have recognized the limitations of their own thinking and the blinders they wore in their own selfishness? Likely not, for they first would have to acknowledge that they were but characters in a story, and the control of their destinies being in the hands of another.

The same desperate selfishness consumes the world today. Christmas time, the time of year when we celebrate our Author entering His story to redeem His characters, is also the season of greatest loneliness and depression for many people. And this tragic subplot will continue to be told so long as people fail to recognize they need saving.

But there is hope – great hope. At the time of Jesus' birth, an old man named Simeon held Jesus' tiny body and prophesied through the Holy Spirit, "Sovereign Lord, as you have promised, you may now dismiss your servant in peace. For my eyes have seen your salvation, which you have prepared in the sight of all nations: A light for revelation to the Gentiles, and the glory of your people Israel." (Luke 2:29-32) This same Holy Spirit is moving throughout the earth right now, convicting hearts and directing wayward characters to their divine Author. In Joel 2:28-29 God promises about the last days, "I will pour out my Spirit on all people. Your sons and daughters will prophesy, your old men will dream dreams, your young men will see visions. Even on my servants, both men and women, I will pour out my Spirit in those days." People are receiving Jesus in greater numbers today than ever before and having the tragic plots of their lives experience a surprising twist for the better. We have very nearly arrived at the end of His Story, and we know that all will be reconciled and restored in the end. The evidence of His goodness is all around us – so why do we still doubt? As followers of Jesus, may we allow His saving power to illustrate our lives and further develop us as characters in His Story, in order that we may demonstrate His love to a world on the brink of eternal tragedy. For only in heaven can we be assured of living happily ever after!

This week, take time for story time. Read a novel with a happy ending or watch a Christmas movie. Journal freely about the plot, setting, characters, and events, reflecting on what would have happened if the characters decided to take matters into their own hands or the writer entered the story in disguise. Let your imagination soar like a child again, allowing it to fully celebrate Jesus choosing to break into our time and space disguised as a baby. Merry Christmas!

The Magi Mystery

Advent is all about anticipation. It is meant to be a season of hope, preparation, and watchfulness. This sense of anticipation was certainly evident in the magi, or the three wise men. Matthew 2 tells their story: how they had followed a star from the east to Judea and brought gifts to worship the newborn king of the Jews. What a journey that must have been, and what joy they must have felt when they found him! But have you ever wondered who these men really were and how they knew what the star meant?

The Magi came from Persia, which had formerly been Babylon during the time of the Jewish exile. The magi were priests of the Zoroastrian religion well-studied in astrology, directly descended from the astrologers Daniel had served centuries earlier. Because of Daniel's prophesies, they knew approximately what year the Messiah would be born (Daniel 9:25) and because of Daniel's legendary conduct and piety, they were prepared to go and worship Daniel's King, a king foreign to them.

You see, four hundred years earlier, Daniel was a teenager taken by force from Israel to serve as a slave in the court of Babylon. He was probably confused, lonely, and scared. Yet he chose to live from inner conviction rather than concede to the new cultural practices he was now surrounded with. Though respectful of royal court authority, he chose to remain loyal to his supreme King, the Lord Most High, and was subsequently esteemed by both God and man. God gave Daniel knowledge and understanding of all kinds of literature and learning, and he could understand dreams and visions. Combined with a trustworthiness and diligence in both character and duty, Daniel held a significant position of influence among the pagan astrologers in the royal court for the remainder of his life. Even as vain kings, jealous satraps, and sabotaging officials came and went, Daniel remained unmoved in his convictions and conduct, daily devoting himself to prayer. And so, four hundred years later, descendants of those same astrologers hoped, prepared, and watched for a sign of Daniel's prophesied Anointed One.

We now know that the star they saw rising was the planet Jupiter, which those astrologers associated with royal births. Jupiter is recorded to have 'risen in the east' on April 17, 6 BC within the astrological constellation of Aries the Ram, which those astrologers associated with Judea. What a moment that must have been! Their hopeful watchfulness now rewarded, all that remained was to prepare for that journey of a lifetime!

How ironic that God would reveal his sign to *pagan astrologers* instead of to the Jews! Yet Isaiah 60:1,3,6 poignantly declares, "Arise, shine, for your light has come, and the glory of the Lord rises upon you! [...] Nations will come to your light, and kings to the brightness of your dawn. [...] Herds of camels will cover your land, young camels of Midian and Ephah, and all from Sheba will come, bearing gold and incense and proclaiming the praise of the Lord." You see, the coming of the magi was a fulfillment of prophecy and symbolized the access all non-Jewish people now have to the throne of God. Now *all* those who prepare a place for God's Son in their hearts and anticipate his second coming can experience eternal life! And it was all because of a Jewish slave named Daniel who refused to compromise his faith in the Lord Most High. Through his private diligence in prayer and public diligence in duty he influenced an entire pagan nation and left a legacy that continued to resonate with them four centuries later. Without Daniel, seeing the sign of a foreign King's birth would have meant very little, yet their response indicates a deep connection. As polytheists, it could be argued that their pilgrimage served merely to appease a foreign deity, but I feel their joy in seeing the star suggests otherwise. Not only do Daniel's writings contain precise prophecies of the Anointed One to come, but detailed accounts of personal encounters Daniel had with 'the Son of Man' in dreams and visions. The fact that they offered gold (royalty), frankincense (deity) and myrrh (humanity) indicates their understanding of the uniqueness of this King God Man and their desire to worship Him. The testimony of Daniel – like your testimony today – had such a profound influence on seekers around him that it changed history. So ask yourself, what influence is your life having on the culture and people around you? Do you believe one person's life can truly have an impact centuries after they're gone? We only have to look at Jesus' life to answer that question; a life that was watched for and heralded by pagan men longing for truth, and one that continues to change lives today.

This advent season, remind yourself that we are still hoping, preparing and watching for Jesus' coming – the second time. His light that broke into our darkness two thousand years ago is still spreading across the earth, and our testimony and influence are the tools He uses to spread that light. This week, reflect and journal on what you want your influence to be as you prepare to celebrate His birth and herald his return. The world will be a brighter place because of it.

LIFE AS WE KNOW IT

I'd like to introduce you to someone. Her name is Crystal. She is like the rest of us in every way but one: she is an unborn baby. If Crystal could talk to us about life as she knows it, what would she say? That there is no such thing as light or air, cold or hunger, and that legs are only good for kicking?

We might try to convince her that she can look forward to experiencing sunlight and breathing fresh air; that her dark chamber of fluid is only a tiny dimension of a world much greater than she could ever imagine. We might try to prepare her for the time to come when she will experience cold and hunger; that this restrictive space she currently resents and pushes against is designed for her protection and nourishment. We might try to inform her that the arms, legs, and features of her body that right now seem to have little or no purpose were given to her as an assurance of the life that is to come. That her present reality is only temporary, preparing her for an existence that will be entirely different.

Finally, we might try to point her to Mother: a higher being that she can't see, yet who surrounds her life right now and who promises to care for her in the next. That the coming cold and hunger will simply be the means of showing Crystal her absolute need for Mother, uniting them spiritually rather than merely physically as now. All of this would be incredibly difficult for Crystal to believe. The here and now is all there is or could ever possibly be, she would say. And Mother? What a strange and illogical concept!

Our lives outside the womb could also be described as merely 'life as we know it.' For just as a crystal needs a specific temporary environment to form in solution, so we as humans were put here on the earth to grow into the likeness of God's Son Jesus within the environment He has given us. As difficult as it may seem to believe, this life is not all there is; we only inhabit a tiny dimension of a world that makes up true reality. All our suffering, frustration, and pain is meant to instill in us a need for our Heavenly Father and unite us to Him in an eternally secure bond of love that transcends the physical realm. The faith He gives us now is our assurance of a life to come with Him, when our faith will truly be our sight.

I chose this analogy for the Christmas season because it takes on even greater wonder and significance when you imagine God himself choosing to become a human fetus. As incredibly humbling and limiting as being a human adult is, there is certainly an added dimension of hindrance and confinement inside the womb. Yet God sent His Son to earth as an infant for the specific purpose of experiencing all the ordeals of mankind, including a humble birth and torturous death.

Because Jesus entered this world as a baby, we now have this opportunity to celebrate His birthday, and to rejoice in the wonder of our own rebirth through Him. For Jesus told us, "no one can enter the kingdom of God unless they are born of water and the Spirit. Flesh gives birth to flesh, but the Spirit gives birth to spirit" (John 3:5-6). Just as a child in the womb must be delivered in order to experience more abundant life, so also we need to accept spiritual birth in order to have the eternal life God desires for us. Naturally, it requires using different senses of perception and operating in a different mechanism than before, yet life as we know it on earth is merely a temporary prenatal state. The limitations of this world are just the confinements of a womb serving to develop and mold us into the children that Father God wants to produce. Having faith in the unseen and trusting in the provision of God surrounding you is the training ground required for the after-life that awaits. So may you reflect this Christmas on the miracle of birthThe second insisted,

"Well I think there is something and maybe it's different than it is here. Maybe we won't need this physical cord anymore.", and particularly the wonder of Jesus' coming from heaven through a mother's womb. The rebirth He now offers your spirit will bring you forth into a life that is greater than you could imagine. The first replied, "Nonsense. And moreover if there is life, then why has no one has ever come back from there? Delivery is the end of life, and in the after-delivery there is nothing but darkness and silence and oblivion. It takes us nowhere."

This week, reflect on the unique in utero environment, with both its limitations and provisions. Remember, a baby's fingerprints are formed through its interactions with the womb's inner surface; as it reaches and pushes against its environment, its unique identity is formed. How is your current season of struggle shaping you personally for your destiny? Take time to journal your thoughts for humans experiencing the confinements of a prenatal state right now, both physically and spiritually.

Give My Heart

What can I give Him, poor as I am?
If I were a shepherd, I would bring a lamb.
If I were a wise man, I would do my part.
Yet what I can I give Him - give my heart.

Christmas is all about giving - every year we busy ourselves with finding that special gift for that special someone. Yet how much do we really consider what it means to give, and how we give to God? Particularly at Christmas, for whose birthday is it, anyway?

I remember when I was six, I recited the above poem in our school's Christmas pageant. I didn't feel the full weight of the words then, only that I had to say them from memory. Yet because of that exercise, these words by Christina Rossetti have not only stayed with me but have become a part of me. Being deeply shaped by both our good and bad experiences is something unique to each childhood, causing many adults to wish they could either forget or revisit those years. Despite the emotionally-charged memories we all now carry, God wants to help us as adults come to terms with how our past has shaped us, and to live in a healthy balance between responsible maturity and genuine childlike vitality.

The Bible instructs us to come to Jesus as little children (Matthew 19:14), and it's easy to understand why. Children are more trusting than adults and are more deeply impressed and shaped by their experiences. In those first formative years, our hearts were open to the world. Life brought us to tears one minute and laughter the next. We also had a different view of giving. Children give hugs; children give a picture they made; children sing songs or tell a story as a gift. Jesus delights in these offerings from the heart. Yet somewhere along the journey of life, our resources of time and talent became neglected in favour of money and things when we consider giving a gift.

How poignant, then, that it is at Christmas when we try to see the world through the eyes of a child once again. This year, may we make an extra effort to give like one. Make a priority of reflecting on what the Lord's birthday means to you and let your imagination direct how you could approach gift-giving differently. And once Christmas is over, may we all remember that Jesus longs us to have that same childlike heart of love for Him every day of the year. He delights in a heart that is generous, impressionable, and sensitive to His voice. It will be the cheapest as well as the most expensive gift you will ever give.

This week, reflect on your childhood Christmas memories, and that anticipation you felt beforehand. How might you recapture that childlike joy and wonder this year? How might you shower your love more fully onto your Saviour, giving your very heart as your gift to Him and to those around you? Meditate on these things as you create your Christmas list, praying for ideas and opportunities to honor His heart inside you.

Fit for a King

I have been an admirer of Catherine, the Duchess of Cambridge, for many years. In a world that seems to praise those who embody immorality and rebellion, the Duchess is a rare jewel that models courage, compassion and faithfulness in an elegant and modest package. Once, I began to imagine making a gift for the Duchess. I enjoy designing clothes and so lingered in that thought for a moment. However, where would I begin? How might I create something truly unique? What would she most enjoy receiving and find the most useful? Would it even be accepted amongst all the other offerings and gifts that surely are presented to her daily from people around the world?

First, I would need to create a detailed design. Then I would select the finest materials to make it with. Lastly I would carefully bring my design concept to life, paying close attention that every step is perfectly executed. Throughout the creation process, it would be entirely an offering of admiration with no strings attached, in an attempt to honor someone worthy of receiving my best.

These imaginings made me reflect on what we give to God. Since we're in the season of gift-giving, do we ever meditate on the substance of our offerings to Him, and our motives behind the gift? Do we take the time to ensure the ingredients are of the highest quality? What about our attention to detail as we bring the offering together? The point is not about perfection, but about honoring someone worthy of our best. As our King, God surely deserves far better than our skill could ever hope to achieve, yet he delights most in a generous and humble heart. (And the office of His kingdom accepts all offerings and gifts, turning no one away!)

A good verse to illustrate this is, "From everyone who has been given much, much will be demanded, and from the one who has been entrusted with much, much more will be asked" (Luke 12:48). What skills, talents, and resources have you been given? If you've been given much, pray the Lord would give you wisdom to properly steward what you have, and live generously. If you've been given little, be trusting and thankful, and offer what's in your hand. It's amazing how he can take the smallest of offerings and multiply it for his glory when it's offered from a pure heart of love.

This reminds me of the song, "The Little Drummer Boy", which tells the fictional tale of a poor boy wishing to give a gift to the infant

Jesus. Though in the presence of resplendent magi and their expensive tokens of homage, the boy offers all he has: a song played on his drum. He plays his best for Him, and the baby Jesus smiles in return. So how does one create a gift fit for a king? It's the love flowing from one's heart that really counts.

To me, this book has been just such a worthwhile labour of love. What I owe my Savior cannot begin to be expressed in these pages. I hope as you've read through this book that you've found it helpful and insightful, and you can join with me in wholehearted admiration and worship to our Lord and King. For it is only in Him that "we live and move and have our being" (Acts 17:28). It's only because of His presence that this narrow path we walk is restricting yet comforting; lonely yet deeply relational; steep yet ascending, winding yet adventurous, painful yet fruitful, rough and rocky yet solid and secure. It's not about where you are, it's Who you're with (and where He's taking you!)

Have a blessed new year!

Looking Back...
Looking Ahead

Reflect on this past year by reading over your journal.

    How have you grown in your knowledge of God and of yourself?
In what ways did God answer your prayers?
What worries and fears came to nothing?

    How did you find relief and comfort in surrendering your plans, feelings, and fears to the Lord through prayer and through writing them down?

    Finish your journal by writing about your anticipations for the coming year, and then intentionally commit once again to giving Him all your love, all your life.

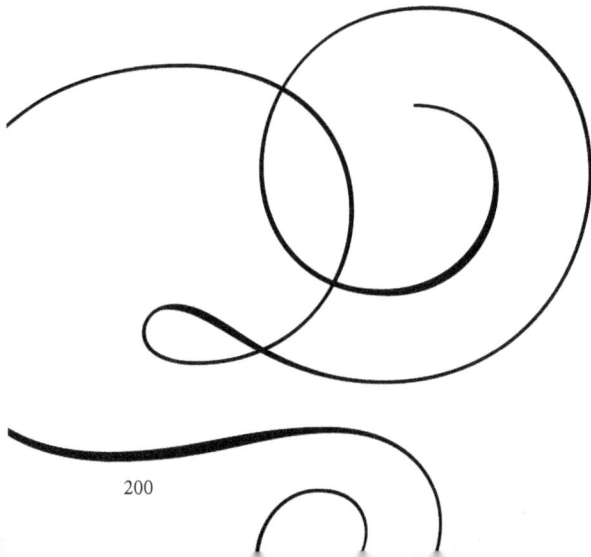

Original Poems

I hope you've enjoyed this devotional journal journey! I thought I would end our time together with some original poetry. I love how we've been partnering this year with the Lord and with each other. If this devotional has blessed you, consider buying a copy for a friend, and be sure to go back and read what you wrote down in your journal last January! You will be amazed at how the Lord has worked in your life and how He has revealed to you more of Himself and more of who you are through Him. God bless you!

Woman of God

> You formed my every part
> Your love pursued me right from the start
> Each moment I have to live
> You knew before time how many You'd give
> Early will I study Your word
> And into the night will I pray
> For You have placed me here on this Earth
> To hear Your small voice and obey.
>
> I want the world to see
> they can have their lives set free
> I want the world to see
> how they can live abundantly
> I want the world to see
> the beauty of Jesus in me
> the beauty of Jesus in me
>
> You clothe your daughters with honour and strength
> So we can help others in need.

May loving hearts consume all our days
and wisdom and peace we receive.
I want the world to see
they can have their lives set free
I want the world to see
how they can live abundantly
I want the world to see
the beauty of Jesus in me
the beauty of Jesus in me

Let your compassion flow
through motivations pure as snow
as women You've called us to be
extensions of Your hands and feet

Remember

When busyness leads me astray
And our cord of communion frays
My heart starts to fear
I forget you are near
And again You must bring me to say

I choose to remember
Your unfolding plan,
the gifts from Your hand.
I choose to remember
the ways You have spoken to me.

You know the state of my heart
How the world can tear it apart
Only You can hold it secure
When I ask You to keep it pure.

Waiting on the Lord

The times of Earth are in Your hands
The seasons change by Your command
I bring my prayers to the foot of Your throne
When answers will come cannot be known

I'll wait, I'll wait on the Lord
When a moment to me is eternity
I'll wait, I'll wait on the Lord
Till Your plan I can finally see.

The closer I draw, the nearer I feel
Your unfolding plan is becoming more real.
Fulfillment will come as I cling all the more
Now that faith has grown deeper than ever before.

I'll wait, I'll wait on the Lord
When a moment to me is eternity
I'll wait, I'll wait on the Lord
Till Your plan I can finally see.

You promise Your best to unwavering souls
Who live each day with hope as Your story unfolds
Trusting and asking for purpose each day,
Your blessing and favour will brighten my way.

Recommended Reading

66 Love Letters - Dr. Larry Crabb
A Woman's Secret to a Balanced Life -Lysa Terkeurst
Anticipatience -Sharon Virkler
Becoming a Woman of Influence -Carol Kent
Becoming a Woman who Listens to God -Sharon Jaynes
Becoming Myself -Stasi Eldredge
Becoming the Woman of His Dreams -Sharon Jaynes
Captivating -John & Stasi Eldredge
Designing a Woman's Life -Judith Couchman
Fight Like a Girl -Lisa Bevere
Having a Mary Heart in a Martha World – Joanna Weaver
Lady in Waiting -Debby Jones & Jackie Kendall
Love as a Way of Life -Gary Chapman
Nurture -Lisa Bevere
Prayer Warrior –Stormie Omartian
Secrets of an Irresistible Woman -Michelle McKinney Hammond
Set-Apart Femininity -Leslie Ludy
Sister Freaks -Rebecca St. James
Teaching Kids Authentic Worship -Kathleen Chapman
The 5 Love Languages -Gary Chapman
The Jesus I Never Knew -Philip Yancey
The Power of a Praying Wife -Stormie Omartian
The Resolution for Women -Priscilla Shirer
Transforming Children into Spiritual Champions -George Barna
Twinkle -Elisa Morgan
Wait for Me -Rebecca St. James
What Happens When Women Say Yes to God -Lysa Terkeurst
What To Do Until Love Finds You -Michelle McKinney Hammond
What's So Amazing About Grace? -Philip Yancey
Your Heart's Desire -Sheri Rose Shepherd

About the Author

Ruth-Ellen grew up in Hamilton, Ontario, Canada, graduating from Redeemer University College with her B.Sc. in biology in 2003.

She then spent many years studying and working in the field of women's health, which enabled her to develop a clearer vision for how she could best help women find their unique potential in the Lord. Observing the abuse and neglect that the female heart often suffers as women seek fulfillment and value, Ruth-Ellen felt compelled to begin writing down thoughts and insights that would bring hope and help ease the pain of those around her. Returning to college to pursue deeper Biblical instruction, there Ruth-Ellen was further equipped with the additional skills and insights she needed to bring this work to completion. She completed a B.A. in Biblical Studies in 2016.

Outside of writing and teaching, Ruth-Ellen enjoys singing, leading worship, playing the clarinet, scrapbooking, following the British Royal Family, photographing nature, knitting and crocheting, and watching old movies.

All photos in this book, including the cover photo, were taken by Ruth-Ellen.

www.ingramcontent.com/pod-product-compliance
Lightning Source LLC
Chambersburg PA
CBHW050901160426
43194CB00011B/2250